FREE BOY

FREE

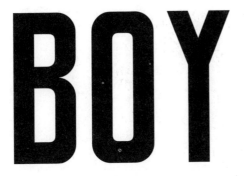

BOY

A True Story of Slave and Master

LORRAINE McCONAGHY

JUDY BENTLEY

V Ethel Willis White Books

UNIVERSITY OF WASHINGTON PRESS
Seattle and London

This book is published with the assistance of a grant from the V Ethel Willis White Endowed Fund, established through the generosity of Deehan Wyman, Virginia Wyman, and the Wyman Youth Trust.

UNIVERSITY OF WASHINGTON PRESS
PO Box 50096, Seattle, WA 98145, USA
www.washington.edu/uwpress

LIBRARY OF CONGRESS CATALOGING-IN-PUBLICATION DATA
McConaghy, Lorraine.
Free boy : a true story of slave and master / Lorraine McConaghy, Judy Bentley.
    pages cm—(V Ethel Willis White Books)
Includes bibliographical references.
ISBN 978-0-295-99271-6 (paperback : acid-free paper) 1. Mitchell, Charles, born 1847—Juvenile literature. 2. Fugitive slaves—Washington Territory—Biography—Juvenile literature. 3. Child slaves—Washington Territory—Biography—Juvenile literature. 4. Blacks—British Columbia—Victoria—Biography—Juvenile literature. 5. Underground railroad—Washington (State)—Puget Sound—Juvenile literature. 6. Tilton, James, 1819–1878—Juvenile literature. 7. Slaveholders—Washington Territory—Biography—Juvenile literature. 8. Surveyors—Washington Territory—Biography—Juvenile literature. 9. Slavery—Washington Territory—History—Juvenile literature. 10. Washington Territory—Biography—Juvenile literature. I. Bentley, Judy. II. Title.
E450.M673M35 2013   306.3'62092—dc23   [B]   2012044637

For the last two or three years, a number of black ingrates around here have been constant in their endeavors to bring about a rupture between Charlie Mitchell and his benefactors, holding out the delightful prospect of becoming a **free boy** by running away from his master and making his escape to Victoria.

—*Olympia Pioneer and Democrat*, September 28, 1860

CONTENTS

FREE BOY

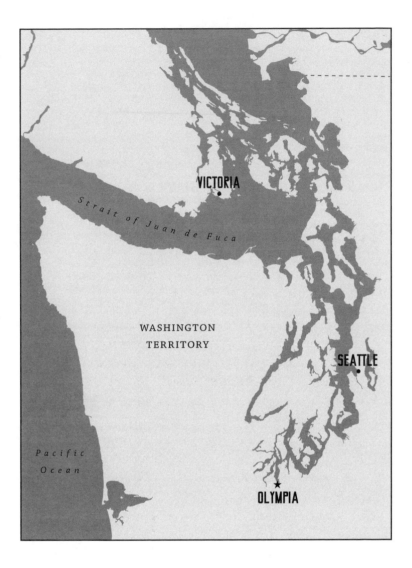

PROLOGUE

OLYMPIA, WASHINGTON TERRITORY, SEPTEMBER 23, 1860

A light-skinned black boy hurried along the muddy streets of Olympia, Washington Territory, a hatbox hooked under one arm. The yells of teamsters on Main Street, the crack of whips, and the rattle of wagons faded away as Charlie Mitchell ducked quickly into an alley. Charlie leaned into the shadows on the wall and closed his eyes. He needed quiet, and he needed time to think.

Charlie was 13, a slave belonging to the surveyor-general of the territory, James Tilton. It was market day, and he'd been sent to pick up parcels for Mrs. Tilton. Two black men had approached him on the street in front of the milliner's.

"You, Charlie Mitchell," the big man whispered, passing close on the sidewalk, looking hard at him, sideways. "In here." He grabbed the boy's elbow and steered him into the empty barber shop and into the back room. It wasn't the first time Charlie had been back there—he knew what was coming.

With a hand on Charlie's shoulder, the taller man looked at him squarely: "Listen to me! You're a slave, Charles Mitchell, and you don't have to be. You got a choice. You don't have to stay here in this town, this country. You come down to the dock, by the Eliza Anderson," *he nodded toward the bay,* "just before first light, tomorrow morning.*

Jim here's the cook, and he'll be watching for you and hide you on board the steamer. You stay good and hid because when you get to Victoria, all our friends will be waiting for you. You set foot on that dock on Vancouver's Island, and you're free."

"But you gotta decide tonight. We won't come back again. This is too dangerous." The big man looked into his eyes and then released his grip and left quickly.

Once they were gone, Charlie walked out to the street and stole around a corner to be alone. The men had talked to him three times already, always in the barber shop. They seemed so sure that Charlie should be free, should want to be free, should make up his mind to run away. He'd been living with Mr. and Mrs. Tilton for nearly eight years—he almost couldn't remember his own mother, dead and buried at home, at Marengo Plantation on the other side of the world.

He leaned against the wall, still holding the hatbox, and stared straight up into the bright September sky. What did it mean to be a slave? He worked for the Tilton family, but it wasn't a job that he was paid for or that he could quit. He belonged to the Tiltons; they didn't beat him, didn't starve him, but he did what he was told to do. He ate in the kitchen and went to school with half-breed kids. He wasn't a Tilton, wasn't an Indian, but he wasn't really black either. He was a slave because his mother had been a slave; he was born that way. As far as he knew, Charlie was the only slave in Olympia, maybe in all of Washington Territory, but the Tiltons never called him a slave. They just called him Charlie.

The two black men who dared him to run away seemed so sure, so confident. They dressed in suits and waistcoats like Mr. Tilton, but they were really dark, much blacker than Charlie was. Mr. Tilton always told Charlie that it was good that he was so light, like his father. Mr. Tilton said that a lot.

Charlie pushed hard off the wall with his shoulder and walked back to the wooden sidewalk. Mrs. Tilton would be mad if he forgot anything or if he was late. He walked fast down the noisy street, first to the bookseller, whose clerk fetched a bundle of books just in from

San Francisco, then on through town, picking up packages. Everyone called him "Mr. Tilton's Charlie."

So, "Fetch down that box, Tom. Mr. Tilton's Charlie is here." All through town. Charlie carried the parcels home to the fine frame house with a view of the bay and the mountains.

That night he lay awake on his mat in the attic above the kitchen, thinking about the only home and family he knew, good food to eat, a warm place to sleep. He thought of Mr. Tilton's promise, that when Charlie turned 18, he'd be free to go, free to make his own way. If it was true, that was more than four years to wait.

In the chilly dark morning, Charlie quietly left his bed before the cook started the fire. He tiptoed downstairs and stepped carefully over the creaky floorboard. He paused one more time at the door, listening. There wasn't a sound in the house.

Did he wonder, "What am I doing?" And then did he run?

1

JAMES TILTON

The Making of a Master

At the first light of day on a September morning in 1847, Lt. James Tilton crouched outside the high stone walls of Chapultepec castle, waiting for the order to attack. Chapultepec was the last bastion defending Mexico City from the American invaders. If it fell, Gen. Antonio Lopez de Santa Ana and his army would certainly surrender the city and lose the war.

Lieutenant Tilton had rested uneasily during the night, unsure how his company of riflemen would perform. Who would storm the fortress, exposed to fire from the defenders above? Who would be the first up the ladders? Overnight, officers had moved among the men, quietly offering promotions and cash to anyone willing to brave enemy bullets to place ladders against the walls and climb over the parapet.

Tilton needed no bribe. At age 28, he was a confident officer in the Voltigeurs, an elite rifle company in the U.S. Army. The Voltigeurs were patterned after the French cavalry, but they fought on foot, carrying the best rifles available. They were often used as sharpshooters to weaken the enemy in advance of the main infantry assault. Tilton wore his distinctive gray uniform with pride, following in the patriotic tradition of the men and women in his family.

It was a fine tradition. During the Revolutionary War, his great-uncle James had served as George Washington's physician. The family treasured a lock of the general's hair, tied with ribbon and given to the doctor. While British soldiers had scoured the streets of Wilmington, Delaware, hunting for revolutionaries, young Tilton's grandmother had boldly sneaked two rebels out of the city, right under the eyes of the redcoats. Grandfather Tilton had fought in the revolution and earned a medal for his courage from the Marquis de Lafayette, a keepsake passed from eldest son to eldest son. Grandfather Gibson had smuggled cannons through the British blockade of Chesapeake Bay during the War of 1812.

So when President James Polk called for American patriots to fight against Mexico, James was eager to join up. Critics claimed that the war was a pretext to extend slavery in the Southwest, but that charge didn't bother the young man. A restless, determined ambition drove the Tiltons, generation after generation. James Tilton was the third in his family to bear the same name and the same belief in the country's destiny. He was ready to distinguish himself and eager to extend the American empire.

The first summer of warfare in Mexico had been brutal. In June, the Voltigeurs had landed, three hundred strong, at the beach of Vera Cruz and marched inland for weeks through the burning heat. They paused in their relentless push toward Mexico City for battles at Churubusco and El Molino del Rey, which Tilton would remember as the bloodiest battle of the war.

Four evenings later, the exhausted army moved into assault positions beneath the walls of Chapultepec. All day, American cannons had battered holes deep into the masonry walls of the castle, but the defenders had not surrendered. At dawn on September 13, the guns boomed again, but precisely at 8:00 a.m. they stopped—the signal for the attack. An eerie silence fell over the Voltigeurs who would lead the charge. Tilton readied his rifle and checked his cartridge belt.

Tilton's company was the first to rush forward along the south side of the castle. Mexican troops had covered an opening in an outer stone wall with a sandbag bunker, but the Voltigeurs broke through, hastily took cover, and laid a heavy fire on the castle above. The infantry charged across boggy ground and high grass as Mexican cannons sent showers of grapeshot and canisters smashing through the tops of cypress trees below the walls. Limbs crashed and fell as the soldiers ran, yelling and firing, until they stormed over breastworks, reached the outer walls, and took cover.

Once again the yells and thunder paused. Tilton watched from cover as the recruited volunteers hauled heavy ladders and pushed them up against the walls of the citadel itself. Waving regimental flags and cheering, the Voltigeurs scaled the ladders, leading the assault. As Tilton climbed, a Mexican defender's bullet tore across his cheek and up along his forehead, grazing his right eye. Ignoring the pain and the streaming blood, Tilton thrust himself over the wall and flung out the colors in triumph. After a brief rest, Tilton wiped the blood from his eyes and led his company along the causeway into Mexico City. The Mexican forces regrouped and fought back fiercely, but their general surrendered the city the next day, effectively ending the war.

Tilton made himself at home in Mexico City, one of 160 American officers who organized the Aztec Club—to play cards, drink, dine, and recover from their wounds. Gen. Winfield Scott honored the heroism of the officers who formed the club, praising their courage: "You have been baptized in fire and blood, and come out steel," he told them. Tilton had joined his generation's military elite, which included an officer who would become the U.S. president—Franklin Pierce.

Like many of that elite, James Tilton supported the American imperial mission. Rather than waste time worrying about disagreements at home—slavery and race—they believed that the United States should expand aggressively throughout the continent, spreading the "experiment of liberty." Tilton and others had no doubt that it was the destiny of the United States to stretch across the continent, to seize land from any peoples who were in the way, and to become the benevolent masters of races they considered inferior.

The journalists and politicians back home were exultant that the Mexicans had been decisively beaten, but most veterans hated Mexico—the heat and the flies, the starving dogs, the whining beggars, the corrupt officials, and the Mexicans themselves who seemed servile and lazy. Tilton was eager to leave Mexico behind. The United States had gained new territory—Texas, Utah, Nevada, California and parts of Arizona, New Mexico, and Colorado—completing a national pathway across the continent to the Pacific. As the huge Mexican cession came under the U.S. flag, Tilton was ready to take America's measure—surveying it, laying it out, and setting it down on a map.

James knew early in his life that he would become a surveyor. He was born at the estate called Tilton Hill in Wilmington, Delaware, in 1819. His father, Dr. James Tilton, had grown up in a family that owned a few slaves, but he had left the land to study medicine. He worked as a doctor at the famous Dupont gunpowder works, but when land opened up for settlement in the new west, Dr. Tilton saw opportunity for himself and his sons. He started a medical practice in the bustling city of Madison, Indiana, splayed out on high bluffs above the Ohio River. Side- and stern-wheelers steamed up the Mississippi and Ohio, bringing coffee and spices from Asia to the port. Great mounds of coal, cured pork, and cotton waited on the levees along Front Street for export. The new state promised fame and wealth to determined men in return for their hard work.

On the western edge of the United States, everyone was claiming land. Treaties signed with the Indians opened land to settlers who would homestead. Surveyors spread out over the woods, meadows, and hills with their transits and compasses, plotting an orderly grid for homesteaders' claims. States and territories were surveying their boundaries, building canals, roads, and railroads. At the young age of 14, James entered the state service of Indiana as an assistant engineer and rose rapidly in the ranks.

While his son surveyed Indiana, Dr. Tilton dabbled in land speculation. The state legislature had authorized construction of a railroad from Madison to Indianapolis, the new capital in the middle of the state. Anticipating the first station ten miles north of Madison, Dr. Tilton bought eighty acres of prime farmland and platted a town there in 1836. He named it Dupont in honor of the French family he admired. The Tilton family moved north to a home in the brand-new town, anticipating the railroad boom.

Out in the countryside near Dupont, the nation's ongoing argument over slavery turned local. To the southwest, antislavery settlers organized the Neil's Creek Abolition Society. They founded an antislavery church, boycotted slave-produced goods, and assisted fugitive slaves to escape pursuit on Indiana's Underground Railroad. With money from eastern abolitionists, they founded Eleutherian College and promised to educate black and mulatto children. Local opponents burned down the student dormitories, but the academy persevered for several years.

This vicious opposition was centered just a few miles away, southeast of Dupont. The Latta Tavern on Middlefork Creek was a meeting place, a "castle," for a chapter of the secret society known as the Knights of the Golden Circle. The Knights wanted to create an American slaveholding empire, with Cuba at the center. Armed and dangerous, they threatened violence against abolitionists, harassment of free blacks, and capture of runaway slaves.

Living in the same township as both abolitionists and the Knights, Tilton's parents walked a careful middle ground. Over several generations, the Tiltons and the Gibsons had lived and prospered in border states in the uneasy space between slave and free—in central Delaware, eastern Maryland, and southern Indiana. Indiana was a free state and slavery was prohibited there, but Kentucky—right across the Ohio River—was a slave state. Madison's free black community offered secret havens for runaway slaves who risked their lives for freedom, swimming the river by night to reach the Indiana shore.

The Tiltons in Delaware and the Gibsons in Maryland had owned slaves. Slavery was part of everyday life in America for millions, as was the threatened status of free blacks. Freed slaves had little education and few family connections to help establish them in the world. Instead they became indentured or apprenticed workers, trading their labor in exchange for training in a trade. After moving to Dupont, Dr. Tilton apprenticed a 9-year-old black boy, John Smith, and promised to train him as a farmer until he reached the age of 21. The boy owed his labor to the Tilton family for twelve years, without pay.

Dr. Tilton's death in 1840 put an end to his great plans for Dupont. Two years later, funds ran out for the railroad, which had hardly advanced beyond the town. Indiana's poor financial condition closed ambitious public works projects, ending the younger Tilton's job in 1842 and leaving him footloose. James Tilton returned home briefly to settle the estate to support his widowed mother, and then he set off around the world. James joined the U.S. Navy and served as a captain's clerk and then as purser, keeping accounts on several warships, from 1842 to 1845, visiting Africa and China and circumnavigating the world on the USS *Perry*. The restless young man had to get something out of his system—maybe conflict within the family, maybe a failed romance, maybe the loss of his father.

Once back in the States, he returned to surveying to earn his living. In the next few years, the life of a surveyor took him to boundaries between the territories of Iowa and Minnesota, to townships in Missouri and Mississippi, and to explorations for the transcontinental railroad from the upper Missouri to the upper Mississippi rivers. He was in Washington, DC, reporting the results of a land survey, when the United States declared war against Mexico, and Tilton gained an officer's commission in the Voltigeurs, an experience that would shape his political and racial views for the rest of his life.

James Tilton returned home in the summer of 1848 to barbecues celebrating the American triumph. Given a hero's welcome, he was 30 years old, seasoned from travel and combat. He had shed blood under "the flag of the Union," and his loyalty to the country was unwavering. But in little more than a decade, the conflict over slavery would split the nation and unravel Tilton's world.

Just a month after he returned from the war, in August 1848, James married Isabella Hanson Adams. Isabella, called Belle, grew up in Cincinnati, just up the river, but their families had known each other in Delaware. James's and Isabella's maternal grandmothers, Lydia and Nancy Hanson, were sisters—it was Lydia who smuggled her future husband out of Wilmington when it was occupied by the British during the Revolutionary War. A relative of Isabella's father was a signer of the Declaration of Independence. Coming from such renowned families, the couple returned to Wilmington to marry, at Trinity Church.

They settled down in Dupont, long enough for James to join the local Masons. He applied for a military pension, citing his eye injury and acute rheumatism he had incurred from chilly nights on guard duty. The couple's first child and only girl, Fannie, was born in 1850, and a son, Edward, in 1852; both babies were christened in Christ Episcopal Church in Madison.

When he was home between work assignments in the field, James would have escorted Belle to brilliant social balls in the dining room of the new Madison Hotel. Out of earshot of the women, heated political discussions warmed the reading room on winter evenings. The Mexican War had raised the specter of the possible expansion of slavery to the Southwest. Then the Compromise of 1850 admitted California to the Union as a free state but gave slave-holding states the right to track runaway slaves to free states. The Fugitive Slave Law gave Kentucky slave-owners the right not only to track down runaways who crossed the Ohio River but to force Indiana law officers to assist the pursuers.

Faced with such deep divisions over race and slavery, James Tilton became increasingly active in politics, as did many Americans in the decade leading up to the Civil War. In the presidential election year of 1852, Tilton campaigned hard for the Democrat Franklin Pierce, whom he had met at the Aztec Club. Pierce was a northerner who was willing to uphold the constitutionality of slavery in order to preserve the Union and avoid civil war. This conviction matched Tilton's fierce loyalty to the country and willingness to tolerate slavery. Although Pierce was little known in Indiana, he won the state handily with the help of advocates like Tilton.

A year after his election, President Pierce appointed his fellow Democrat and war comrade, James Tilton, to the position of surveyor-general in the newly formed Washington Territory. Pierce said the appointment was motivated not by politics but by his respect for Tilton's professional skill. Tilton's surveys would resolve the land claims of the Hudson's Bay Company and establish the boundaries of Native reservations, under the treaties. He would survey routes for wagon roads and railroads and establish homestead boundaries for the settlers who were streaming west on the Oregon Trail. Like his grandfather and father, Tilton was restless and ambitious, eager to prove his worth on the next frontier.

James and Belle Tilton packed their bags and said their goodbyes, bundling up little Fannie and Edward, Irish cook Mary Garity, and Tilton's widowed half sister, Clara, and her two sons. The eight travelers prepared for a grand adventure, bound for distant Washington Territory, months away by river steamer and sailing ship, around Cape Horn and into the Pacific Ocean. But first, James Tilton had obligations. He had to pay a visit to his mother's family in Maryland.

Tilton stood up and stretched, straightening his back. The sun had just risen over the Indiana hills, filling the window panes with gold. He bent down and blew out the flame in the lamp and cocked his head to one side, looking critically at the drawing laid out on the table. His drafting instruments lay neatly alongside the drawing board, and his surveying tools and backpack leaned against the wall. Tilton was plotting a careful survey map from his notes. It had to be just right.

He was working in the front parlor of the family home in Madison, on a temporary desk. The chilly room was stacked with crates filled with books, linens, and china, all ready to be shipped to far-off Olympia, Washington Territory. Belle Tilton walked softly through the door and stood behind her husband. She put her arms around him, turning him toward her, away from the drawing.

"Aren't you tired out, Jim? You've been working all night."

He smiled at her. "The final draft is done, and I wanted to finish it before we leave. I will be very busy with Aunt Mary and Cousin Rebecca, and then we'll be at sea."

"But how is your eye? Does it pain you?

"Yes," he said reluctantly, "it does. Almost all the time, and when I'm tired, I can't see very clearly."

"Are you certain that taking this appointment in Washington Territory is a wise move?" Her words began to tumble out. "Such a wild, uncivilized place to raise the children, far from my family and your brother and sister, thousands of miles from anywhere, Indians and cougars, and the work will be so hard for you—"

"Belle, I have no wish to spend my life sitting at a desk," Tilton said firmly. "That's not where the real opportunities are—this is the chance we've been waiting for, to be posted to a fresh, new country in the West! We can pick the very best land before the railroad gets there, and the land surveyor will be the most important man in the territory.

"But," he said in a different tone, turning away. "We've been through this before."

"Yes, I suppose we have. . . . And this trip to Maryland?"

"I owe it to them."

2

CHARLES MITCHELL

The Making of a Slave

Cholera spread swiftly along the Eastern Shore of Maryland in the summer of 1850. Warm, brackish pools dotted the marshlands bordering the fields; the sultry air lay heavy on the earth. The epidemic moved across the waters of Chesapeake Bay and reached Marengo, an estate on a long neck of land. Mistress Rebecca Reynolds Gibson lived at Marengo with her mother and thirteen slaves. The great house had burned a few years before, leaving just outbuildings to shelter the white women and their slaves. There was a new baby in the cramped quarters and 3-year-old Charles Mitchell, a boy of mixed race.

Charlie was born on a failed plantation where whites and blacks had lived for more than 150 years. The fields around Marengo and the slaves that tilled them had supported a bountiful way of life for the Gibson family. The first Jacob Gibson in America was a Scots immigrant, a blacksmith who acquired land in the late 1600s from the earnings of his trade and from an opportune marriage. He soon bought slaves and became one of the wealthiest gentleman planters in Talbot County, growing tobacco.

Charlie's mother was descended from those slaves. Her family had come through the horrible Middle Passage from Africa, to the slave market of a nearby town. There, these black men and women were sold, bought, and brought captive to Marengo. Slaves worked the Gibson land in the hot, humid air, planting, weeding, and harvesting tobacco leaves. Tobacco soon wore out the soil, however, and many Maryland plantation owners shifted their acreage to wheat, supplying bread for soldiers' rations during the American Revolution. The wheat market remained strong after the war, and the blacksmith's grandson, also named Jacob Gibson, expanded the farm, renting fields and putting his slaves to work nearby. Fired with revolutionary zeal and admiration for the French, Gibson named the family plantation Marengo, after an Italian village where Napoleon Bonaparte had triumphed. Gibson called himself Citizen Jacob and named his son Lafayette—shortened to Fayette—after the marquis who had aided Americans in their rebellion against Great Britain.

Despite his radical enthusiasms, Citizen Jacob was known locally as a man of high temper and violent passions. He told his overseers to punish field hands harshly if they did not work hard or fast enough. Of the thirty-four slaves living at Marengo in the early 1800s, half worked in Gibson's fields—doing backbreaking manual labor from sunrise to sunset. The rest were house slaves who washed and ironed, cooked and polished, and waited on the Gibson family. For many generations, the names of these slaves, their birth and death dates, and the names of their children were unrecorded.

The first names of Marengo slaves appeared on an estate document after Citizen Jacob died in 1818. They included "a man called Joshua, a woman called Phillis, . . . a woman called Phillis Lewis, . . . a boy called William, a boy called Peter, a man called Harry, a woman called Cassiah." More than thirty years later, the first Maryland slave census listed thirteen slaves at Marengo, but it recorded only age, race (black or mulatto) and gender—not name. A black female listed as aged 80 and a man and a woman aged 60 could have been Charlie's family. The two women listed as ages 25 and 23 may have been his mother and his aunt.

Charlie's mother worked in the big house at Marengo all her life, serving as Rebecca Gibson's personal maid ever since both were girls. The two young women knew each other well, knew one another's habits, voices, and emotions. Somehow the maid met Charles Mitchell, a white man who worked on the oyster boats that plied Chesapeake Bay; she gave birth to a son in about 1847. Although she could not marry Mitchell, the slave mother gave her son his father's name. Perhaps she loved the father; perhaps she simply hoped the white name would give Charlie a future. No one wrote down the date of his birth. Most of Charlie's life would be lived unnoticed, except for one big moment.

As an infant and toddler, Charlie lived in a household struggling to survive on a shrinking plantation. When Rebecca's grandfather Jacob died, he left a tangle of debts to be sorted out by his sons, Fayette and Edward, during a period of economic depression in Maryland. Neither son was a successful farmer. They were forced to sell two slaves, Peter and Cassiah; large numbers of livestock; and more than five hundred acres of land to raise cash to pay the bills. By the time Charlie was born, Fayette and Edward had died, and the big house had burned. Of the remaining slaves, only two were males of working age. By 1850, Marengo was a world of women, black and white, living together on a ruined plantation as cholera moved across the waters.

Rebecca Gibson began hearing about the fearful death toll in the cities on the inland side of Chesapeake Bay. From southern ports, the epidemic had spread to towns on the Ohio and Mississippi Rivers, to wagon trains leaving from St. Louis on the Oregon Trail, and all the way to the gold camps of California. In the morning a victim might have a slight stomach ache; by noon she would be vomiting, wracked by diarrhea; by afternoon, dehydrated with a raging fever; and by evening, she would be dead.

One morning, Charlie's mother awoke with the unmistakable signs of the illness. The only treatment Rebecca could give her was hot lemon water and honey or, if she sent for the white doctor, he would have prescribed calomel or laudanum. Nothing helped. As vomiting and diarrhea turned to a raging fever, the victim's face grew blue and pinched. According to family accounts, Rebecca asked the dying maid what she could do for her.

"Take care of Charlie," was the reply.

"I will."

Rebecca Gibson promised she would, but how could she keep that promise? When his mother died, Charlie Mitchell was only 3 years old. Because he was born to a slave mother, he was a slave, bound for his lifetime to the Gibson family. One day, Charlie might be an asset to Rebecca, but not now, not in Marengo's hard times. Western wheat was cheaper and better than Maryland wheat, and local plantation fields lay fallow. There was little money left to support a child who was too young to work or send on errands across the Miles River, to the town of St. Michaels.

Some of her neighbors sold their slaves south to work in the cotton fields, and Rebecca likely sold her two remaining male slaves while Charlie was still a toddler, but she wouldn't sell Charlie. Some compassionate owners were freeing their slaves, but Charlie was too young to be set free on his own, and Rebecca couldn't afford to free another slave as his guardian. Rebecca's grandfather, Citizen Jacob, had grandly proposed founding a local bank whose profits would set free all of the slaves in Talbot County, but his proposal came to nothing. The Gibson family inherited his ambivalent views about slavery, but they also inherited his slaves—they condemned slavery in the abstract but practiced it every day.

Facing increasing threats of being sold south, some Maryland slaves took their lives into their own hands. Frederick Douglass escaped from a harsh master on a nearby plantation to become an abolitionist leader in the North. Harriet Tubman saw her sisters sold south as young girls, and when she was able, she left neighboring Dorchester County and fled to Philadelphia. Lonesome for her family, she sneaked back to lead more than one hundred fugitives along the Underground Railroad from counties in Maryland to freedom in the North. Maryland slaves escaped at the grave risk of being caught and punished and sent back to far crueler slavery. Given the danger, no one put Charlie Mitchell on the Underground Railroad.

Charlie's white father couldn't help either. He was a free man, but he likely had little more power than a slave. Nothing more is known of him than his name, race, and occupation as a waterman. He was probably a descendant of indentured servants, transported from England for their labor. Mitchell may have been shanghaied by a shipping agent who received $200 for each worker produced, or he might have been recruited from a jail or workhouse in Baltimore. He may have met Charlie's mother with the help of a black cook who served on the oyster boat. He may have loved her; he may have raped her; he may not have known about the birth of his son. Even if he did, there was little he could do to help unless he could afford to buy Charlie, if Rebecca Gibson had been willing to sell.

There was one more option—the Tiltons. For more than a century, the Maryland Gibsons had been marrying the Delaware Tiltons who owned land just across the border, on the Duck Creek Hundred. Dr. James Tilton had married two of Citizen Jacob's daughters, in succession, and his sister had married a Gibson son. With such intertwined families, the Tiltons visited Marengo often for holidays, weddings, and business. Unlike the Gibsons, the Tiltons were no longer tied to the land or to owning slaves. Instead, the Tilton men were professionals—doctors and surveyors. Not rooted in estates or slaves, they thrived on family connections and the opportunities offered by the expanding American frontier.

By 1853, when Charlie Mitchell was 6 years old, Rebecca Gibson couldn't hold Marengo together any longer. She and her mother sadly gave up and sold the estate, moving into a small house in St. Michaels. Rebecca likely sold any remaining slaves except for one servant and the boy: the black slave named Becky and the little boy named Charlie Mitchell. She could not make up her mind what to do with him.

Living together in the crowded household, the Gibson women received a letter one day from Rebecca's cousin James Tilton. He wrote excitedly that he had accepted a presidential appointment as surveyor-general in Washington Territory. Suddenly, Rebecca saw how she could keep her promise: she decided to give Charlie to James Tilton, to take to the far Pacific Northwest with his family. Rebecca was freed of her obligation to her dying slave, Charlie's mother, and of the responsibility of caring for Charlie. And Charlie Mitchell would have a new life far from Maryland.

One account says Rebecca gave Charlie to her cousin as a gift, even as a belated wedding present; another that he "rented" the young boy; yet another that he "employed" him. No matter Charlie's official status, Tilton agreed to take care of the boy, a responsibility he added to his growing family. For Tilton, it was a favor to Rebecca. For Charlie, trusting James Tilton was the only choice he had.

The night before he was to leave, Charlie sat on a low stool next to his aunt, leaning against her legs. The oil lamp cast a circle of light on the two. She was sewing quickly in the warm kitchen, taking small tight stitches, trying to make two decent outfits for Charlie to take with him.

"Aunty Becky?" he whispered. "I don' wanna leave here. Why I gotta go?"

The black woman tightened her mouth. "Don't do no good to pine. You lucky, gettin' away from this place. Missus is doin' the best she can, the best she know how, sending you out west with Master Tilton. You gonna go on a big ship, sail to San Francisco. Your ma wanted you to have a good life. You gonna get that, in the West."

Big tears welled out of Charlie's eyes. His mother had died too fast, before she could tell him where to find his daddy. He had a daddy somewhere, he was sure, named Mitchell like him. He meant to find him someday.

"Don' want no good life, no big ship—I just wanna stay here with you. I'll work extra hard. I'll be good, I promise." Charlie turned his

head, pressing his face into her skirt. The woman laid down her sewing and rested a hand on his head.

"Charlie, honeylamb. It's nothing to do with good or bad. You gotta go. But one day, you come back here. You come back and see me. Don't you never forget."

"I won't, Aunty Becky," he promised, little knowing how far away he would travel.

3

GROWING UP WITH THE TERRITORY

On a chilly spring day in 1855, James Tilton strode down to the dock in the frontier town of Olympia to greet his family arriving on the steamer from San Francisco: his wife Isabella, daughter Fannie, toddler Edward, sister Clara and her sons, his half brother Edward, the Irish nurse Mary Garity, and lastly the boy Charlie. Tilton must have been uneasy about bringing Charlie to the "free territory" of Washington. As the patriarch of the extended household, he never thought twice about indenturing an Irish servant, taking care of Clara's boys when their father died, and finding jobs for his brothers and cousins. He'd taken responsibility for Charlie Mitchell, too, but the boy was different—a slave in Washington Territory, a place not clearly slave or free.

Named grandly for the mountains to the west, Olympia was a primitive town on a narrow peninsula jutting into Puget Sound. Like Charlie, most people arrived by boat at the long dock built out over the tidelands to deep water. The tide rose and fell fourteen feet, twice each day. Cedar canoes lined up on the beach, and Indian women gathered clams. Two dozen wooden buildings straggled along Main Street, a rutted wagon road ankle-deep in mud. Lush forests surrounded the town, and schooners sailed to Australia, Hawaii, and San Francisco, carrying spars, masts, and lumber from Puget Sound sawmills. Prospectors hunted for gold, silver, iron, and coal in the mountains to the east. Washington Territory was rich and raw, ideal for a man seeking his fortune.

The two families, the cook, and the slave boy settled into one household, and Tilton returned to work. He had hurried north from San Francisco, ahead of his family, to start his job as surveyor-general. After just two weeks, he was a person of influence in the young capital. Most men in southern Puget Sound farmed or worked for wages in the coalfields, in the woods, or at the sawmill; some were hands on the schooners and steamships. Many sought government appointments. Every significant office in the territory was filled by an appointee, chosen by the president from among political loyalists. That's how James Tilton became surveyor-general and how Isaac Ingalls Stevens became governor—they were appointed by President Franklin Pierce, in gratitude for their service during his election campaign and in the Mexican War. In turn, Stevens and Tilton and other members of the "Olympia Clique" filled lesser positions with their own cronies.

In the first few months of 1855, Tilton hired half a dozen men and put his brother Hanson and half brother Edward on his payroll. Accurate maps were vital to the territory's future, and Tilton plunged into his professional responsibilities, planning road and railroad surveys and drawing maps that would allow settlers to claim homesteads. Tilton's job was political as well as technical. His office would challenge the claims of the Hudson's Bay Company, the British firm that had preceded Americans in the Pacific Northwest. It was Tilton's job to settle the boundaries of the Hudson's Bay property, which would determine how much compensation the company received.

Tilton's work seemed at first to be just a matter of engineering, drawing accurate lines and features on maps. But his surveys faced an immediate problem: the Willamette Meridian had been established in Oregon, intended to extend northward into Washington Territory as a baseline. However, the meridian projected into Puget Sound—literally out into the water. Instead of extending the Willamette Meridian, Tilton established a brand-new north-south line on the Washington mainland. Confident and stubborn, he was displeased with the rebuke he received from his superiors in Washington, DC: "All the proceedings in regard to your intended Puget Sound Meridian are illegal, null and void." Tilton was ordered, instead, to conform to the Willamette Meridian. Despite his irritation, he complied.

Tilton earned a good salary from his work, and his family lived well. They attended Episcopal services, and Tilton at once joined the Olympia Masonic Lodge, to which Isabella presented a lock of Gen. George Washington's hair, "a gift well authenticated." As soon as she recovered from baby Bayard's birth, the Tiltons began to entertain in the tiny circle of Olympia society, hosting dinners for prominent friends like Isaac Stevens, governor of the territory. James Tilton was well-bred and well-off, a man of wide experience. Later, an acquaintance admired him as "a man of soldierly bearing and aristocratic tastes"; another remembered him as a "real southern gentleman."

Charles Mitchell stood out in the Tilton household; visitors noticed and remembered him. He was not the only person of color in town; half a dozen black men and women lived nearby, described in the 1860 census. Alex and Rebecca Howard ran the Pacific House. Jackson Jourdan, Henry Strong, Arthur and Eliza Strong—they were cooks or laborers. George Washington Bush and his wife owned their farm out in the countryside. Bush had arrived with the very earliest settlers, but it took a special act of the territorial legislature to allow "George Bush, a free mulatto" to claim a section of land. Bush had five sons, but they were free. There were no other children in Olympia who were slaves.

Tilton had promised to train Charlie for work as a ship's steward in the new territory. On Puget Sound, small steamships carried passengers, freight, and mail among the little port towns of Olympia, Seattle, and Port Townsend and up to the British Crown Colony of Victoria. Most of the steamers offered meals, and the cooks—or stewards, as they were called—were usually black men. Tilton planned to have Charlie trained as a steward and to free him when he came of age. Tilton later said that Charlie was naturally intelligent and honest and that the boy was educated in schools in Olympia and Steilacoom, likely with Indian and mixed-race children. Charlie was not really a member of the Tilton family, and his status was surely made clear to him in ways that even a little boy could understand. He learned to read, write, and do sums, and after school he ran errands for Mrs. Tilton, tended the garden, and kept the stove and fireplaces stocked with wood in the winter. Maybe he found time to go fishing too.

Charlie's political education occurred on the streets of Olympia and at dinners at the Tilton home. He heard snippets of conversation as guests talked of the states they had left and the issues that reached all the way across the continent. One issue, in particular, dominated the smoking clubs and parlors in the Pacific Northwest.. That issue was slavery. Did the U.S. Congress have the right to decide whether anyone could be enslaved in the territories, or should each territory decide to be free or slave when it became a state? Could Charlie Mitchell be held as a slave in Washington Territory, and who would decide that?

Some argued that slavery was tied to plantation agriculture, that slave labor was "natural" in the South, in the cultivation of rice, tobacco, cotton, or indigo, but made no sense in the Northwest. Slavery expansionists replied that slaves could work in mines, factories, and sawmills anywhere, not just on southern plantations. Portland's *Oregonian* reported on a proposal that Puget Sound mill owners could save money by "buying negroes, bringing them to Washington territory and employing them as lumbermen instead of white men." The Democratic ticket, claimed the *Oregonian*, advocated carrying slavery into the territories. Most westerners thought the issue should be decided by each territory when it became a state, by "popular sovereignty," and that the federal government had no right to impose its will. The General, as Tilton was called, was a staunch Democrat, the party in power in the territory, and on slavery he followed the party line.

The issue in Washington Territory that was closer in place and time, however, was the right of American settlers to claim land. Among the first tasks of territorial governor Stevens was to legitimize land claims by confronting the Native Americans who had lived on the Northwest's land and traveled its waterways for centuries. The Squaxin and Nisqually people camped on the shoreline of Budd Inlet, sharing the space with the new settlements. They fished the waters of the Sound and rivers and traveled by canoe as far north as the Strait of Juan de Fuca and as far south as the Columbia River. In December 1854, Governor Stevens had negotiated his first treaty with them, the Treaty of Medicine Creek, at a Nisqually council ground just east of Olympia. Gathered tribes ceded more than two million acres and agreed to move to much smaller reserves of land.

Or so it seemed at first. Charlie heard rumors on the streets of Olympia that Chief Leschi was not happy with the treaty. How could his people subsist on a small bluff above the Nisqually River, separated from the river delta and source of their food and wealth? The more Leschi understood the boundaries Stevens had set, the less he liked them.

Leschi was not alone in his discontent. Prospectors chasing gold crossed Indian land without hesitation, provoking a response. Word filtered west across the Cascade Mountains of miners and hunters, and even the federal Indian agent, found dead, killed by Indian warriors. Throughout the summer and into the fall of 1855, as Charlie settled into school, tensions grew. The territorial legislature, meeting a few blocks from the Tilton home, sent an anxious appeal back to Washington, DC, requesting federal military protection. Native people vastly outnumbered settlers in Washington Territory, and it was just a matter of time before Indian resistance spread to Puget Sound.

Worried that protection would not come soon enough, in October 1855 Governor Stevens ordered western Washington settlers to form a volunteer militia to protect their homes and families. He appointed James Tilton as adjutant-general because of his Mexican War experience. The following day, October 15, Tilton took a steamer to Seattle, to borrow enough muskets and ammunition from a U.S. Navy warship to arm about one hundred men. Both sides prepared to fight about who owned the land and who was in charge.

For more than two hundred years, newcomers to America had fought Native people. From first contact, some Europeans tried to eradicate Indians and others tried to "civilize" them, but every European wanted to own Native land. They believed they deserved to. Europeans saw Native Americans as members of an inferior race. In Mexico, James Tilton and his fellow officers had reached the same conclusion about the Mexican people. Most white Americans also saw black people the same way, as people to be taken care of or mastered. Territorial settlers thought they should care for Indian people as misguided children or suppress them as savages.

Events moved quickly that fall. A few days after the call up of militiamen, a small unit known as Eaton's Rangers began guarding the Cascade passes to prevent Yakama and Klickitat raiders from joining the uprising on Puget Sound. When a small patrol went out on horseback to scout an Indian fishing camp near the White River, they were ambushed, and four men were killed.

"Hell is broke loose [in Washington Territory]," James Tilton wrote grimly to a friend. Settlers were angry and frightened, and families fled their isolated farms, crowding into Olympia. Town residents met to plan their defense against Indian attack and decided to build a stockade and blockhouse under Tilton's direction. The stockade extended across the peninsula, bay to bay, with the blockhouse at the corner of Main Street and Fourth, defended by a cannon. Everyone in town worked frantically on the construction, including Charlie Mitchell, only 8 years old.

Like the rest of Olympia's residents, the Tilton family abandoned their home and moved into temporary housing behind the barricade. At the worst of the crisis, the settlers begged the captain of a lumber schooner to keep his ship in port at the Olympia mill, in case they needed a fast escape into Puget Sound. Olympia became an armed camp under siege as refugees huddled behind the stockade. By night, the nearby woods seemed filled with menace, and distant hooting owls or barking dogs startled the jittery lookouts.

When the attack came, Indians chose Seattle, not Olympia. In January 1856, a coalition of Native warriors from throughout the territory attacked the tiny settlement, which was even smaller than Olympia. Settlers rushed to blockhouses, and the warship *Decatur*, moored in the harbor, successfully defended the town with its carronades. Two months later, General Tilton issued a call for one hundred more men to join the militia. "Fort Tilton" was built at the western side of Snoqualmie Pass, base camp for a small force that watched for bands of Indians passing in either direction. Out in the backcountry, militia patrols encountered small groups of Native warriors, and men murdered one another in vicious, bloody encounters. Tilton struggled round-the-clock to coordinate the widely scattered, poorly equipped militia companies.

Charlie returned to school, but some of his friends were missing. "Half-breed" children, whose fathers were Hudson's Bay Company men and whose mothers were Indian or mixed race, stayed away from Olympia. During the Treaty War, their farms and families were not attacked, and Governor Stevens was convinced that they were helping hostile Indians. He demanded that they leave their homes and move into custody. When some refused, he ordered them arrested as collaborators.

Charlie heard that Tilton supported the governor's decisions, telling his militia company to arrest all "suspected persons . . . [in] the theater of war." Tilton was loyal to Stevens and went so far as to forcibly remove a U.S. marshal from the governor's office when Stevens was threatened with contempt of a judge's order. Tilton referred to the Indians as savages and professed himself "delighted" when militiamen massacred sixty Indians at Grande Ronde in July 1856. Tilton had no doubts about the rightness of Governor Stevens's actions or about his own leadership during the Treaty War.

By January 1857, the war was over in western Washington, but settlers wanted revenge for their friends and family members killed in the fighting. Chief Leschi, war leader of the Native forces west of the Cascades, was arrested and charged with murder. At a meeting calling for Leschi's execution, Tilton called the Treaty War a "war of races," in which Indians intended to "exterminate the white man." Leschi's first trial ended with a deadlocked jury, the second with a conviction and a sentence of death.

Everyone in Washington Territory had a strong opinion about Leschi's trials and his sentence. In general, settlers who considered themselves Democrats supported Governor Stevens and his vengeful stance; Republicans opposed Stevens on principle and argued against Leschi's execution. The U.S. Army officers serving at Fort Steilacoom were convinced that the verdict was mistaken and the sentence illegal—that Leschi had been a legitimate combatant during a state of war and could not be charged with the civil crime of murder.

On a February morning in 1858, Leschi's sentence was carried out. Fort Steilacoom commandant Silas Casey refused to permit the hanging to take place at the fort. A gallows was built about a mile east, out in the lonely prairie, where a crowd of men and boys gathered. Nisqually drums pounded steadily from the distant prairies.

Leschi was escorted by thirteen men on horseback, his hands tied in front of him, a square-built man with a heavy jaw. The sheriff and his deputies dismounted and helped Leschi down from his horse. He paused at the foot of the rough ladder and then climbed firmly to the scaffold and turned to look at the men assembled, his dark brown eyes piercing the crowd. He was asked if he wanted to confess to his crimes, and he shook his head. He bowed to the crowd, and then he spoke slowly in his own language, saying that he was ready to die and had made his peace with God.

When he finished, Leschi nodded. A dark hood was pulled down over his head, hiding his eyes, and he stood still as the noose was placed around his neck. At 11:35 in the morning, February 19, 1858, the platform was dropped and Chief Leschi was hung.

With the war over, the Indian treaties were enforced and James Tilton returned to his ambitions, full of energy and plans. The year before, in 1857, he and other territorial settlers had joined residents of six other northern states and territories to incorporate the Northern Pacific Railroad. And in the fall of 1858, after two years of work, Tilton published a meticulous survey of Washington Territory west of the Cascades, showing its vast potential for settlement and development, especially if the railroad came through.

Believing the maps, James must have convinced Belle, in quiet conversations by candlelight, that the future of this rough frontier was bright. He requested reappointment as surveyor-general, and the territorial legislature—with only one dissenting vote—agreed. President James Buchanan complied on June 19, 1858. The Tilton family moved into a spacious new house up on the hill in Olympia, with a commanding view of the Sound. James Tilton was determined that his family's fortunes would grow up with the country.

Charlie's fortunes, however, were less certain. The hanging of Chief Leschi must have intensified his uncertainties about how he fit into a town where he was the only black child, free or slave. Just south of Olympia, however, on Bush Prairie, lived another child of mixed race. Lewis Nesqually Bush was free, and his father, George Washington Bush, was a mulatto like Charlie. The elder Bush was prosperous—not only prosperous but a friend of the Nisqually since the days when his wagon train had first arrived on south Puget Sound. His youngest son, Lewis, was born in Washington and was given a middle name that honored the tribe and the place.

Charlie Mitchell and Lewis Bush were fishing on a lazy afternoon, one sunny Sunday in October 1858. They didn't expect to catch much, were just fooling around, sitting on a big rock in the creek.

"Lewis?"

"Yup?"

"We're friends, right?"

Lewis threw a pebble in the water, trying to hit a floating leaf.

"Yeah, sure, we're friends, Charlie. Why?"

"Well, you got that Nisqually name, and Mr. Tilton, he don't like Indians."

"Yeah, well, my dad says Stevens's men got that hanging wrong. Leschi was only defending his people. That wasn't murder . . . Say, how come General Tilton has that Indian kid named after him if he hates Indians so much? That son of George Pickett, that army man up on San Juan Island, and his squaw."

"What kid?" Charlie sat up straight. "I never heard of no Indian Tilton."

"That one Mr. Pickett named James Tilton Pickett."

"Never happen. Mr. Tilton wouldn't let nobody name some half-breed kid after him. No way."

Lewis turned to look at Charlie, face-to-face. "I'm named after an Indian, and I'm a half-breed kid, just like you, just like him. Just a different kinda breed, is all." They stared each other down, then started laughing.

"Still, it don't make sense," said Charlie, casting his fishing line upstream. "James Tilton Pickett. What a crazy thing. Must be a joke."

"No joke, you and me. Just the way things are."

4

CHARLIE'S CHOICE

As Charlie turned 11 in 1858, he made his way around town with confidence. He ran errands and picked up packages at Bettman's general store, Willard's apothecary, and Louisson's shoe shop. As he walked along Main Street, he passed the Washington Hotel and, farther along, the Pacific House. Now that he was older, Charlie's home chores had changed, and he kept the stove and fireplaces stocked with wood in the winter and tended the vegetable garden in the summer. Everything the Tiltons couldn't grow in that garden, Charlie picked up in town—coffee, tea, sugar, rice, and spices from ginger to cinnamon. The town was less rough, less raw than when he first arrived. The big blockhouse was still standing on the town square, but the stockade was gone; Indian canoes were scarce. There were lawyers' and government offices, and the *Pioneer and Democrat* printing office was a busy place, with knots of men arguing politics.

At the dining table, in the living room, out on the porch, and downtown at the newspaper office, everyone was talking about the brand-new *Dred Scott* decision. If Charlie wondered where he fit among the Indians, whites, blacks, and half-breeds of Washington Territory's complicated racial society, this ruling by the U.S. Supreme Court told him—and his master, James Tilton—what to think. The court had ruled in the case of a slave named Dred Scott that even if Scott was brought to a free territory, he was still a slave. Slaves like Scott and Charlie were not citizens but items of property, and no one—not even the U.S. Congress—could interfere with the owners' constitutionally guaranteed property rights, their "right to property in a slave." An American's property was his to keep, and he could own his slaves in a territory until a majority declared for or against slavery at statehood, exercising their "popular sovereignty." Rebecca Gibson had thought she was sending Charlie to a free territory that would become a free state, but overnight, Washington Territory was no longer free soil.

Even free blacks in the Pacific Northwest might have cause for worry. Oregon had barred slavery in its constitution when it moved from territory to statehood in 1859, but Oregon voters had also barred free blacks by an even greater margin. Oregon voters did not want slavery, but they did not want to compete with free black labor or associate with free black families either.

A few settlers and army officers had freed their slaves when they arrived in Washington Territory, and there were a few free black men and women scattered throughout the Northwest. There were also rumors about black slaves held here and there. The *Dred Scott* decision meant that James Tilton could continue to own Charlie until he freed him or until Washington voted to become a free state, in the distant future. The boy could wait it out or he could run away. As he grew older, Charlie understood that choice. But where could he go? And who would help him get there? His fortunes began to turn with discoveries north of the border.

In 1858, settlers in Washington Territory were thrilled by the exciting news of the gold strikes along British Columbia's Fraser and Thompson rivers. Spurred by glowing newspaper accounts, hundreds of would-be miners streamed through the territory from California and Oregon and raced north, traveling in canoes, schooners, and steamers. An energetic, ambitious man could

make a fortune selling coal to the Puget Sound steamers and outfitting and entertaining the prospectors along the way. James
Tilton was just such a man, and he had been waiting for just such
an opportunity. He embarked on a risky, ambitious scheme.

Tilton hoped to strike it rich, but he also had to meet his
growing obligations. A number of cousins and in-laws had traveled west to join the Tiltons in Olympia, hoping for adventure
and needing to be fed and housed. He and Belle had a new baby
of their own, Howard. Then his good friend, George Pickett,
had named Tilton the guardian of his infant son, born to his
Native wife. The baby was named James Tilton Pickett in honor
of the men's friendship. The northern gold rush came at the
right time.

Eager to share in the boom, Tilton invested in a development
venture 150 miles north of Olympia at Sehome. Tilton and two
partners opened a coal mine, platted the townsite, and promoted
the Bellingham Bay Trail as a quick and easy overland route to
the gold strikes. They hoped that the trailhead at Bellingham Bay
would become a gold rush boomtown. Tilton wrote optimistically to a friend that his cousin "Ned Gibson is here, having just
arrived from Fort Hope [on the Fraser River], for more provi-
sions. He reports about 400 miners at work, making from a half
to two ounces per day per man. He brought down 70 ounces."

But critics pointed out that Tilton and his partners' so-called
Bellingham Bay Trail was no more than a line drawn on a map
through some of the roughest country in the Northwest. The
Puget Sound Herald optimistically reported that one of Tilton's
partners was out surveying the route. But in June 1858, the part-
ner sent a cautious letter back to Olympia: "Don't send anybody
out on the trail until I report it through. I have made two unsuc-
cessful attempts to get through but the snow prevents. . . . I shall
make another effort." The effort failed. Tilton's Bellingham Bay
Trail never succeeded, but he continued to make strategic business and real estate investments.

The real gold rush action was in Victoria. Most miners

bypassed Puget Sound and Bellingham Bay on the way to the mines and headed straight for Vancouver Island. The Crown Colony of Victoria boomed, situated on a fine harbor on the island's southern tip. When the gold rush began, there were fewer than five hundred settlers in that little town—very like Olympia. But once the news had electrified the world, boatloads of newcomers steamed to Victoria, eager for food, shelter, riches, and fun. Never before, according to an eyewitness, "was there so large an immigration in so short a time into so small a place." In just six weeks, 223 new buildings were constructed in Victoria, and prospectors lined up outside the Hudson's Bay Company store, willing to pay exorbitant prices for every necessity from boots to bread.

If Charlie felt alone in Olympia, he would not have felt alone in Victoria. Among those flourishing in the boomtown were ambitious African Americans who had been drawn first to a similar gold rush boom in California and then to Victoria. In the free state of California, they had hoped to make a new life, but they found stubborn racial prejudice against all blacks, slave or free, and were denied the right to vote and the protection of law. Teenaged Archy Lee was a case in point. Lee was brought as a slave into California and might have expected to be free, but his master hired him out and kept his wages. When his master decided to return to Mississippi, a slave state, Lee escaped. But he was captured and charged under the Fugitive Slave Law. When Lee sued for his freedom in the courts of California, his efforts were met with insults and injustice. As a black slave, he was considered property, not a person.

Faced with such hostility, leaders of San Francisco's black community began to search outside the United States for a place to build their lives. They found it on Vancouver Island. In 1858, thirty-five black San Franciscans visited Victoria, met with a warm welcome, and were encouraged by the opportunities of the Fraser River gold rush. Wellington Moses sent a letter back to California that was passed hand to hand and read aloud: "All the colored man wants here is ability and money," he wrote in excitement. "[Victoria] is a God-sent land for the colored people."

Mifflin Gibbs agreed: "There was ever present [in California] ... the disheartening consciousness that while our existence was tolerated, we were powerless to appeal to law for the protection of life or property when assailed. British Columbia offered and gave protection to both, and equality of political privileges. I cannot describe with what joy we hailed the opportunity to enjoy that liberty."

Three hundred black men and their families sailed to Victoria in 1858–59, leaving behind the America of Bleeding Kansas, the Fugitive Slave Law, and the *Dred Scott* decision. They made their own future. Freed after his third trial, Archy Lee hurried north to join them. Black-owned businesses thrived in Victoria—Peter Lester and Mifflin Gibbs set up a general store in competition with the Hudson's Bay Company, selling flour and spices, bacon and sugar, oysters and pickles. Samuel Ringo opened Victoria's finest restaurant. Nathan Pointer opened a clothing store, Wellington Moses a barber shop. Others worked as carpenters, barbers, teamsters, loggers, and cooks, and some tried their luck in the goldfields. Real estate values skyrocketed, and black settlers who had the means to purchase property were very successful. Victoria was not paradise, but it was a more open and tolerant society; blacks had the sense that they were accepted for what they could achieve.

Some of Victoria's black men and women were committed to helping other enslaved blacks find the same freedom they had found. They had helped themselves, they had helped Archy Lee, and they developed a West Coast Underground Railroad to help others. Newcomer William Jerome had briefly lived in Olympia, and he remembered Charlie Mitchell. He told Victoria's Underground Railroad organizers that there was a black boy in Olympia, Washington Territory, who was held as a slave. William Davis and James Allen joined the conspiracy to free Charlie. Allen worked as a cook on the steamer *Eliza Anderson*, which had a regular mail route from Olympia to Victoria. Allen was in a perfect position to contact Charlie and show him the way to freedom.

The plan unfolded as Allen and Davis traveled south from Victoria on the steamer and then found Charlie running errands on the streets of Olympia. They told him he could be free like them. If he came down to the dock where the *Eliza Anderson* was tied up, they would be waiting. Allen said that he would watch for Charlie and hide him on board, down in the galley. They promised to take care of him once he reached Victoria. But Charlie had to decide that night.

Charlie came into the kitchen of the house on the hill, hatbox tucked under one arm, a parcel of books in another, his mind still fretting over the conversation he had just had with two black men from Victoria. The men had seemed so friendly, so confident, so sure of what he should do.

"That you, Charlie?"

"Yes, ma'am." He set down the packages on the kitchen table.

"Well, you've surely taken your time." Mrs. Tilton bustled into the kitchen, carrying little Howard on her hip. The toddler reached out for Charlie and smiled a big grin, but Mrs. Tilton held him tightly. She was different since Fannie had died—talked louder, moved faster, had little patience with Charlie.

"Did you pick up the books? And my hat? Good. Well, we've all eaten; there's your food on the stove. And, don't forget, Charlie—school is tomorrow, and then the garden. There's beans and tomatoes to pick, and it's time to hoe the winter greens. Oh, and we're getting low on kindling and firewood, both—how that old stove goes through firewood . . . "

She juggled the books, the hatbox, and little Howard and turned to leave. Then she stopped and looked more closely at Charlie, who seemed preoccupied with his feet.

"You're growing, Charlie, looks like you'll need new shoes again, and you sure do eat! You know, Mr. Tilton and I have been talking. We've got that Pickett boy to support now, and that Sehome venture didn't pan out—not that it's any business of yours—but maybe you

don't need to go to school anymore, not sure what you're learning there anyway. Some people in town could use an apprentice, and it would get you out from underfoot."

Charlie raised his head slowly and frowned. "But Mr. Tilton promised, Miz Tilton. He said I could learn until I come of age and then he'd find a job for me, and I'd be free."

"You're free enough, Charlie. Haven't we done everything for you? Brought you to a new territory, away from that plantation life? Fed you, clothed you, sent you to school? Best to be grateful," she nodded and swept out of the room.

Charlie walked over to the stove. His supper was warm on the back burner—left from the family's dinner. Pea soup with ham, and there'd probably be bread—yes, there was, and he cut himself two thick slices and buttered them. A big bowl of soup and some bread, and cider. He ate hungrily for a few minutes, staring through the kitchen window. Then he stopped, the bowl half full, the bread half eaten, and pushed the plates away across the wooden table. The kitchen grew chilly, and he stirred up the fire in the stove and added some wood. Then he just let his mind wander, dreamy-like, trying to remember, trying to imagine.

What would it mean to be free?

Charlie had learned a lot, just keeping his ears open around the house. He'd heard Mr. Tilton and his friends talk loudly about "the damn abolitionists," about "nigger-lovers." He could tell they were scornful of this man Abraham Lincoln who was running for president. Maybe everything would change, but Charlie saw and heard prejudice against blacks every single day. He had learned to be on the lookout for certain men and cross the street when he saw them coming along the sidewalk—the ones who called him nigger and told him this was white man's country and to get the hell out. Would it be different in Victoria, in 1860? Or in Olympia, in 1865, when he was 18?

He would decide before morning whether to stay or to run.

5

STOWAWAY

In the early morning, Monday, September 24, 1860, the steamship *Eliza Anderson* hugged the long dock that stretched into the bay in Olympia. The sun wasn't up yet. The crew was busy getting steam up in the boiler and loading the mail and cargo for the run north to Steilacoom, Seattle, Port Townsend, Bellingham Bay, and Victoria. James Allen, the ship's cook, was down in the galley brewing coffee, frying bacon, and making biscuits—getting breakfast ready for the passengers, expected to board within an hour. He seasoned the chickens for roasting and sliced apples into pie crusts, for lunch, and started yeast dough for the next day's bread and rolls.

Allen worked fast, mechanically, listening intently for any sound of Charlie Mitchell. Every chance he got, he climbed up the companionway and glanced uphill into the chilly fog. Allen was a black man whose home was at Victoria on Vancouver Island, and he had a good job as the steamship's steward, but he was also a conductor on the tiny Puget Sound Underground Railroad. He had never in his life done anything like this. He was brave and decisive, a man of conviction, risking his own freedom and livelihood to free another. But he could only do so much. The rest was up to Charlie.

The night before, Charlie Mitchell made the decision that would change the rest of his life. He thought it over; he wished he could ask advice, but there was no one to ask. In the Tilton home, he knew his place and what to do and what not to do. He knew Olympia, knew the people. But he had decided to take a chance, to trust the black men from Victoria who told him there was another life within reach, as a free boy who could make his own way in the world. Before first light, he slipped away from the Tilton home, heading down the hill to the steamboat landing. He stayed off the path, climbing down through the brush toward the water.

Charlie listened to birds calling in the morning air, overlaid by the muffled shouts of men down in the *Anderson's* cargo hold, the steady pulse of the ship's pistons in their cylinders, and the sigh of escaping steam. The Chinese laundryman walked down the path and out onto the dock, carrying clean and folded sheets, towels, tablecloths, and napkins in four baskets, hanging from poles on his shoulders. The first mate yelled for the cabin steward to come fetch the laundry. Then "John Chinaman" walked back up the hill, swinging his empty baskets, and the landing grew still once again.

When the coast was clear, Charlie ran down the dock and jumped on board. Allen had been watching and hurried him down into the steamer's galley; then he shoved Charlie in an open, low pantry and slammed the door. Charlie had never been so excited in his life; his heart was pounding and he couldn't catch his breath. The pitch-dark pantry smelled of potatoes and onions. Charlie lay down to fit the cramped space, and his eyes slowly adjusted to the dim light that was shining through the crack around the pantry door: he saw a jug of water, some food wrapped in a linen dishtowel, a blanket, a container to pee in. Then just plank walls, like a coffin.

Charlie was not the first fugitive slave in America to be contained in coffin-like spaces on ships and wagons, even in boxes shipped through the mail. Large packages marked "This side up" had been known to deliver fugitives from southern ports to Philadelphia, which, like Victoria, was free. Still, it was scary to be locked up in the pantry, and it was hard to stay still and quiet. Charlie knew he just had to wait. William Davis and James Allen—the two men from Victoria—had told him that everything depended on his silence. He had to be patient and wait in the dark for many hours, for nearly two days. The *Eliza Anderson* would stop in Steilacoom and Seattle and maybe at other ports on Puget Sound too. Allen would check on him when he could, but Charlie had to wait until one of them opened the pantry door and told him it was okay to get out. He would be scared and uncomfortable, they said, but at the end—in Victoria—a whole crowd of people would welcome him and take him home. And that's where he would find his freedom, whatever that meant.

As Allen finished frying the bacon, passengers began to board, crossing the gangway to the steamer. Among the passengers on this run were Washington Territory's acting governor, Henry M. McGill, and his son, a boy of 7 years. McGill was "acting" because he was really the territorial secretary who had replaced Washington Territory's appointed governor, Richard Gholson, when Gholson took a leave of absence. McGill was on his way to talk with Victoria authorities about a shared problem—piracy on Puget Sound. His son was along for the ride.

Another traveler ticketed for Victoria stood out—William Davis, the other man who had approached Charlie Mitchell on the street in Olympia. It was unusual for a black man to purchase passage on the steamer, but Davis was well-dressed, quiet, and reserved, and he seemed completely at his ease as the other passengers stared at him. Some of the passengers had booked cabins for the passage; others, like Davis, paid less and made their way to the main cabin, claiming a chair and arranging their baggage. Most sat down to a big breakfast in the dining cabin, but Davis stayed in his chair.

From his dark hiding place, Charlie heard the distant thumps and bangs of heavy trunks coming aboard and then the crash of closing hatches. He heard the shouts and footfalls as the crew cast off the steamer's lines and coiled them on the deck. The steam engine's rhythm pulsed through the ship's timbers as the steamer slowly moved away from the dock. High overhead, the whistle blew farewell, and at 7:00 a.m. sharp the *Eliza Anderson* pulled away from Olympia. Charlie's journey had begun.

The sun rose, turning the water a shining blue tipped with silver as the *Anderson* headed out. In 1860, the wooden steamer was quite new, launched at a shipyard in Portland, Oregon, only two years earlier. The sixty-horsepower steam engine turned huge paddle wheels on either side of the ship. The steamer carried mail, passengers, and freight, and the weekly route ran between Olympia and Victoria, with a dozen stops along the way.

The *Eliza Anderson* steamed out on the ebbing tide, chugging along at about six knots, a little more than six miles an hour. Passing through the channel, the ship made its first stop at Steilacoom, at about 9:00 a.m., discharging and loading passengers and cargo. The survey had just been completed to build a military road to link the forts at Steilacoom and Bellingham, and sections of the trail were in use. But in 1860, travel by water was still much easier and faster than travel by land. After stopping at Steilacoom, the *Eliza Anderson* headed north, threading between the islands and the mainland, Mount Rainier and the Cascade Mountains to the east and the Olympic Mountains to the west. The steamer passed some Native canoes hauled out on shore and left a wake that lapped up onto the pebbly beaches. In the day cabin, the passengers relaxed in their chairs, reading their books or glancing through newspapers—Olympia's *Pioneer and Democrat*, Port Townsend's *Northwest*, or the *Victoria Colonist*.

At noon, the passengers were called to lunch and sat at tables in the dining cabin, where two waiters served them. They enjoyed the roast chicken and apple pie that James Allen had prepared, chatting and watching the scenery slowly pass by outside the windows. In the day cabin, William Davis pulled out a cold lunch from his carpetbag. He ate it slowly and then went out on deck to lean on the rail and stare south along the steamer's wake, back to Olympia.

Hidden in the warm, dark pantry, Charlie Mitchell smelled the chicken and ate some bread and drank a little water. Some of the passengers dozed off after lunch, taking a nap in their staterooms or in the comfortable cabin chairs. Exhausted by the emotions of the past two days and lulled by the throbbing engine, surely Charlie slept too, his body curled up to fit the pantry space.

The *Eliza Anderson* continued north, making her way through the narrows with the tide. She rounded Point Defiance and headed up the east side of Vashon Island, past Alki Point into Elliott Bay. The steamer docked with a jolt at the tiny settlement of Seattle. Desertion from Fort Steilacoom was common, and Puget Sound ships were routinely searched for runaway soldiers who were trying to escape life in the U.S. Army. But on September 24, 1860, while looking for an army deserter, the searchers in Seattle instead found Charlie Mitchell, a fugitive slave.

The Fugitive Slave Law obligated authorities in every state and territory to return runaway slaves to their owners, wherever they might be. Once he had been discovered, Charlie became the responsibility of the *Anderson*'s captain. When the captain confronted Charlie in the cramped space of the galley, he recognized the boy. Captain John Fleming had been a dinner guest at James Tilton's home in Olympia, and he remembered seeing Charlie there and considered the boy to be Tilton's property.

Fleming decided to teach Charlie Mitchell a lesson, making him work to earn his passage on the steamer and then taking him back to Olympia, back to James Tilton where he belonged. Captain Fleming did not realize at first that *Eliza Anderson* steward James Allen had helped Charlie to escape. Instead, he believed that the boy had hidden on board the steamer all on his own. Questioned by Fleming, Charlie admitted that he had run away from the Tilton home in Olympia, but he did not say that he was expected in Victoria. Charlie kept the secrets of the Puget Sound Underground Railroad—the network of conductors and steamship—while he was standing before the captain. He admitted to being a stowaway, running off on a dare, but no more. So when the *Eliza Anderson* steamed away from Seattle, Charlie was hard at work under the first mate Woodbury Doane's vigilant eye.

Overnight, Charlie slept under lock and key, and on the next day, September 25, he swept floors, made beds, and filled oil lamps, perhaps even doing the dirtier job of shoveling coal, helping the crew member known to the rest of the crew as Indian Jim. Cook James Allen and passenger William Davis would have tried for a few private moments with the boy, to whisper encouragement and advice. But Charlie talked too freely with Rob McGill, the acting governor's son.

Rob sat on the chair, dangling his feet, and stared at Charlie Mitchell. The little boy's eyes followed Charlie's competent hands as he filled the oil lamps and trimmed their wicks, getting them ready for the cabins.

"I know you. You live near us, with the Tiltons. Why did you run away?"

"Didn't run away. Took a dare, that's all." Charlie Mitchell turned the last lamp around, wiping its base as clean as the others. "Just a dare."

"Your clothes are real dirty. So's your face."

Charlie looked down at his shirt and pants, black with coal dust. "Yup, I reckon they are. Shoveling coal's dirty work."

"Why did Mr. Doane talk to you so mean-like? He was plenty mad. Ain't you scared?"

"It don't matter. I don't pay him no mind. I got friends here and I got people waiting for me, going to come to meet me."

Confiding in the little boy, Charlie accidentally revealed his plans. Rob McGill told his father, who informed Captain Fleming.

6

"WRONGFULLY DETAINED"

As the *Eliza Anderson* steamed up to the wharf in Victoria on Tuesday, September 25, a crowd of residents gathered, members of the town's black community and whites who supported their goals—a group of "philanthropic free blacks and English humanitarians," as Olympia's *Pioneer and Democrat* sarcastically described them. These men and women wore their very best clothing, and they planned to bring Charlie Mitchell into their homes and to become his family. They had welcomed other blacks from the United States but never one so young and alone. They waited anxiously and eagerly at the dock, looking out across the harbor at the approaching steamer.

Charlie could not see them; he was locked away. Four hours earlier, he had once again stood before the infuriated captain, who now realized that his cook and one of the passengers had been part of a conspiracy to encourage and aid the flight of a fugitive slave. Captain John Fleming was the absolute authority on board, and he commanded the first mate to lock Charlie into the ship's lamp room and imprison the boy until the ship had left Victoria behind. The lamp room was the windowless storeroom where lamp oil was kept, a fire danger to the ship and its passengers.

Fleming had tried unsuccessfully to flag down other ships heading south into Puget Sound, to transfer Charlie—he didn't want to dock the ship in Victoria with a fugitive slave on board, but he had no choice. Now Charlie was locked up on the *Eliza Anderson*, under the vigilance of first mate Woodbury Doane, "a gentleman in no way well-disposed to the free blacks of Victoria," according to the *Pioneer and Democrat*.

From the *Eliza Anderson*'s pilothouse, Captain Fleming could see the crowd on the wharf. He brought the steamer into the dock, told the engineer to bank the fires under the boiler, and gave the familiar orders to tie up the ship and hoist out the gangway. Many of the steamer's passengers were due to disembark in Victoria, including Acting Governor Henry McGill. As the deckhands carried luggage from the ship to the dock, passengers walked off the steamer and then picked up their bags or hired porters to help them with their trunks. They all hurried up the dock to town, making their way through the excited crowd.

Nearly a hundred people had gathered at the dock, eager to welcome Charlie Mitchell to Victoria. William Davis stepped off the steamer and rushed through the crowd, everyone asking him questions, him not turning aside or saying a word until he got to William Jerome. His news spread quickly: "The boy can't get off the steamer; they've got him locked up!"

They had come so far, and Charlie was very close to freedom. Jerome made a decision. He hurried off with James Allen and William Davis to the law offices of Henry Crease. They had to figure out a way to get Charlie off the ship, and Crease would help them. The attorney was opposed to slavery and would be sympathetic to freeing Charlie Mitchell. Jerome, Davis, and Allen ran to Government Street and burst into Barrister Crease's office.

Captain Fleming also walked off the *Eliza Anderson*, leaving First Mate Doane in charge of Charlie. Doane glared at the milling crowd on the dock and warned them loudly that he "would break open their heads if the attempt was made" to free the boy, according to the *Pioneer and Democrat*. No one left; they all waited.

Meanwhile, Crease listened quietly to the three men asking for help and agreed to take Charlie's case. He questioned them closely in the presence of his secretary, who recorded their observations and knowledge of Charlie and then drafted a transcript of what each had said. Cease asked the three men to swear by their signatures, under oath, that they had spoken the truth. Both Davis and Allen could sign their names; William Jerome made an *X* mark on the document.

These men's affidavits claimed that Charles Mitchell was a slave; that he belonged to James Tilton; that he had tried to run away before but had been too closely watched; that he was trying to escape captivity in Olympia, Washington Territory, United States of America, fleeing to freedom in the Crown Colony of Victoria; that he had stowed away on the *Eliza Anderson*; and that Captain Fleming had locked him in the lamp room to prevent him "obtaining his freedom by setting foot on British soil."

Each affidavit specifically stated that Charlie was "wrongfully detained" on the steamer—that the captain had placed him under arrest and held him against his will. Armed with this sworn testimony, Crease took the affidavit to Chief Justice David Cameron. Cameron considered the evidence and issued a writ of habeas corpus that would free Charlie from the steamer, place him in official custody, and guarantee him due process under English law.

That afternoon, powerful document in hand, Sheriff William Naylor and a Victoria police officer walked through the waiting crowd and approached the *Eliza Anderson* where Woodbury Doane was still standing guard. They tried to serve the writ on the first mate, but he would not accept it. Then Captain Fleming returned, and both *Anderson* officers indignantly protested that the writ was not legal, that British law had no force on an American vessel. But Sheriff Naylor threatened to break into the lamp room and free Charlie himself, and many in the crowd on the dock murmured angrily in support of the sheriff. Fleming quickly consulted with Acting Governor McGill and told him that he feared a riot and bloodshed. McGill reluctantly instructed Fleming "to permit the Sheriff to take the Negro."

When Fleming finally accepted the writ and unlocked the door, Sheriff Naylor took Charlie into his custody. Charles Mitchell stepped off the *Eliza Anderson*, onto the wharf. Most on the dock cheered; some hissed and booed. He walked up the wharf under the protection of the sheriff to spend the night in the Victoria jail, with a court date scheduled for the following morning.

Meanwhile, Captain Fleming fired steward James Allen from the *Eliza Anderson*, telling him that he'd never work on a Puget Sound steamer again. Fleming then walked to the offices of attorney George Pearkes, who handled all the *Anderson*'s legal affairs in Victoria. The captain dictated and swore to an affidavit of his own that formally protested the seizure of Charles Mitchell; the document was transcribed overnight, and Fleming signed it early the next morning, on Wednesday, September 26, 1860. He justified his actions in this way: "Upon the refusal of the undersigned to deliver the Negro, the said Sheriff threatened to force open the room in which the Negro was confined. . . . Whereupon the undersigned to prevent the destruction of property and in all probability much bloodshed opened the door."

Both John Fleming and Charles Mitchell awaited the morning hearing that would determine whether Charlie stayed in Victoria or returned to Olympia. A reporter from the *Victoria Colonist* stopped by the jail to interview Charlie for the newspaper. His attorney, Henry Crease, spent some time with his young client, preparing him for court. Throughout the long afternoon, Charlie looked out at Victoria through his tiny, barred window, seeing everything he could. If he were freed, this would be the place he would live. Outside the jail, the people of Victoria went about their business on foot and horseback in a town much bigger than Olympia. Most passers-by bustled along, but a few people gathered on the wooden sidewalk across the street and stared up at

Charlie's cell. Some waved and yelled encouragement. The devout members of Victoria's community held meetings in churches and homes, praying that Charlie would remain free and stay in their midst.

In the evening, the jailer brought in a basket of the very best fried chicken, biscuits, blackberry pie, and ice cream, home-cooked for the boy by the loving hands of Victoria's black housewives.

"Sure smells good, son. They must like you out there! Here's some hot water and soap, and a towel, so you can clean up a bit. Good luck tomorrow and try to get some sleep. I'll wake you first thing in the morning."

As darkness fell, Charlie heard an unfamiliar song outside the jail window, sung by dozens of voices, in harmony:

> *Praise we the Lord! Let songs resound*
> *To earth's remotest shore!*
> *Songs of thanksgiving, songs of praise—*
> *For we are slaves no more.*
>
> *Praise we the Lord! His power hath rent*
> *The chains that held us long!*
> *His voice is mighty, as of old,*
> *And still His arm is strong*
>
> . . . .
>
> *Praise we the Lord! Let holy songs*
> *Rise from these happy isles!—*
> *O! Let us not unworthy prove,*
> *On whom His bounty smiles*

When their song of praise had ended, the singers dispersed and their lanterns moved away through the dark as they walked to their homes. Too excited to eat or sleep, Charlie lay on his bunk and stared up at the ceiling, thinking about the past two days, the words of the song, and what might happen tomorrow. His future hung in the balance: to stay here in Victoria or be sent back to Olympia. A few wagons rattled by, dogs barked, a distant steam whistle hooted, and then Victoria grew silent in the dark. Finally, Charlie fell asleep, but his dreams were troubled.

7

"A RIGHTEOUS DECISION"

On Wednesday, September 26, after a lonely night in a jail cell, young Charles Mitchell appeared before the Honorable David Cameron, chief justice of the Supreme Court of Civil Justice at Victoria. The case was listed as *Regina vs. Fleming, in re Charles, a slave*, where "Regina" meant Queen Victoria, monarch of the British Empire.

Charles was wearing the same clothes he had on when he left Olympia. Ordered to stand, he stared nervously as the judge entered, wearing a scarlet robe and powdered wig, and mounted the stairs to his bench. "Court," announced the bailiff, "is convened."

Justice Cameron sat high above the courtroom, arranging the papers on his desk, and then gazed out across the crowd. This was not an everyday case. The gallery was thronged with members of the black community as well as many other interested spectators. Attorney General George H. Cary stood and moved that the writ of habeas corpus be properly filed, and then he read the sworn affidavits of William Davis, William Jerome, and the *Eliza Anderson*'s cook, James Allen—three black conductors on the Puget Sound Underground Railroad. Then Cary read aloud the sheriff's own account of the events at the *Anderson* on the previous day. All these documents describing Charles were entered into evidence as he strained to understand them.

Cary opened his argument. He said that Mitchell was a slave who had escaped captivity in a U.S. territory and had fled to British justice. Captain John Fleming, Cary argued, had exceeded his authority in locking up Charles, having no right to hold him against his will on board a vessel docked in Victoria's harbor. Cary argued that Justice Cameron's court had jurisdiction over any ship in British waters and, he continued, if there was any doubt of the court's right to free the slave from the *Eliza Anderson*'s lamp room, well, he was now standing before the court, on British soil. As soon as Charles Mitchell's foot touched the Victoria dock, he was a free boy. Cary carefully built his case, citing numerous English legal precedents: as early as 1772, Lord Mansfield had ruled in the case of *Somersett vs. Steuart* that any slave who entered British territory was free.

Tempers flared in the courtroom when barrister George Pearkes read aloud Captain Fleming's strongly worded protest that the Victoria authorities had no jurisdiction on board the *Eliza Anderson*. Justice Cameron gaveled for silence, to restore order to the courtroom, and he insisted that Fleming be heard. Following the spirit of the *Dred Scott* decision and the Fugitive Slave Law, Fleming described Mitchell as "the property of James Tilton," a runaway who should be "returned to his Master." Fleming argued that Sheriff Naylor had threatened violence, to "force open the room in which the Negro was confined," and that Fleming had reluctantly unlocked the lamp room to prevent bloodshed and damage to the ship. The sheriff's seizure of the boy, Fleming maintained, was a violation of international law. His protest was duly recorded in the court records.

Justice Cameron cleared his throat and gathered the attentive audience in the courtroom with his eyes. He looked down at Charles Mitchell and declared that "no man could be held as a slave on British soil" and that Mitchell's "arrest by Captain Fleming was illegal." Cameron continued, "There being no charge, warrant or commitment against him, I order that the said sheriff do discharge the said Charles from his said custody forthwith." The courtroom erupted with cheers—and a few hisses. The daybook kept at the Victoria jail briefly noted, "A Negro set at liberty." And Charles Mitchell was finally set free and left the courtroom, walking into his future. Captain Fleming and first mate Doane stalked out of the court and down to the Victoria dock. By noon, the *Eliza Anderson* had loaded passengers and cargo and was steaming out of the harbor, bound for Olympia.

It is unclear when James Tilton realized that Charles had run away, let alone escaped to Victoria. In 1860, Washington Territory's telegraph was still four years in the future, and there was no quicker way for news to travel than by steamer. It is likely that Tilton first realized the boy was missing when the family gathered for breakfast on Monday morning, perhaps as the *Anderson* was steaming away from Olympia. But Tilton may have thought he was just out fishing or camping with a friend. It is possible that someone traveled from Seattle to Olympia to let Tilton know that Mitchell had been discovered on the *Eliza Anderson* and that the captain intended to take him to Victoria and then return him to Olympia. It is also possible that Tilton did not learn of the escape until the steamer returned from Victoria.

Whenever Tilton learned the whole truth, he did not cheerfully accept Charlie's choice or Chief Justice Cameron's decision. He thought the boy had made a foolish mistake and was ungrateful for the training he had been given. Most of all, Tilton's rights as a citizen of Washington Territory had been transgressed, and he meant to pull all of the political strings he could to assert those rights.

Four days after the hearing in Victoria, Tilton sent a formal letter of protest to Acting Governor Henry McGill, with carefully chosen language describing his relationship to Charles Mitchell. He stated that "a slave boy belonging to my relative R[ebecca] R. Gibson and for the last 5 years hired and employed by myself . . . was taken by the British authorities from the·mail steamer, by force." Tilton protested Sheriff Naylor's enforcement of the writ of habeas corpus as improper and illegal, a violation of international law, and asked McGill to bring the matter to the attention of the federal authorities in Washington, DC.

McGill did just that, writing to Secretary of State Lewis Cass, in the nation's capital, and enclosing a copy of Tilton's letter. McGill reviewed the events that had taken place on distant Puget Sound: that the *Eliza Anderson* had left Olympia on September 24 and arrived at Victoria on September 25, that the captain had discovered "a slave boy" who was attempting to escape, and that Fleming had locked Charlie up so "that he might be returned to his master." McGill wrote that representatives of foreign governments had no right to board American merchant ships and "interfere" with the ownership of a slave by his master. Until the "voluntary" landing of the slave on British soil, McGill argued that the laws of England "could not dissolve the relation of master and slave" on board an American ship, and Fleming's yielding to the writ of habeas corpus had not been at all "voluntary." If there had been a U.S. Navy warship nearby, McGill concluded that Captain Fleming would have "caused the fugitive to be placed on board" and that the British would not have acted with such arrogance.

Scenting public interest in this explosive story, newspapers in Victoria and Olympia took up the fight. The American editors of the newspapers in Steilacoom, Port Townsend, and Olympia all resented British interference, but they did not agree with each other about Charles Mitchell. Olympia's *Pioneer and Democrat* supported James Tilton wholeheartedly. In fact, Tilton had by then invested in that newspaper and its articles reflected his point of view. According to the *Pioneer and Democrat*, "a number of black ingrates" who were "worthless free negroes from Victoria" had worked hard to alienate the boy from James and Belle Tilton, "who had been to him as a father and a mother." These meddlesome blacks had convinced Charles to become a "free boy, by running away from his master."

After a number of failed approaches, wrote the *Pioneer and Democrat* editor, the boy had finally been persuaded to flee by steward James Allen, "a flashy looking darkey . . . from Victoria." The newspaper recounted how the boy had been given to Tilton by his cousin Rebecca Gibson in Maryland and that he had been deliberately brought to a distant western territory that would one day become a free state. Tilton had promised to educate Charles and train him to earn his living as a steward on a steamer; when he turned 18, he would be freed. Until then, according to the newspaper, Charles Mitchell was not James Tilton's slave but his ward, and Tilton was his fatherly guardian.

Now that the boy had run away, the *Pioneer and Democrat* continued, Tilton was angry and hoped that Charles would not return, "as his services have lately not been equivalent to his expenses." In an interview, Tilton revealed his racial views, telling the newspaper that he considered Charles honest and "naturally intelligent" but judged him unfaithful and ungrateful and "lack[ing] stability . . . as with most mulattos."

Port Townsend's *Northwest* newspaper expressed the general territorial bias against blacks, regretting that Tilton had brought a black boy into the territory at all. The *Northwest* did not support the cause of Charles Mitchell but opposed the presence of *any* blacks in Washington Territory who might socialize with whites or compete with whites for jobs.

However, a Steilacoom newspaper editor saw the events with more thoughtfulness and less partisan passion. A West Coast Underground Railroad was almost inevitable, the *Puget Sound Herald* editor wrote. "Our proximity to the British Possessions on this Coast afford the same facilities to an underground railroad that the Canadas do on the Atlantic." The blacks of Victoria—who had taken their fate into their own hands—were eager to free the slaves of the West. Washington Territory and Puget Sound seemed to this newspaper editor a logical western route to the freedom of Victoria and Vancouver Island.

The newspaper debate mattered little to Charles. The editor

of the *Victoria Colonist* had already met and spoken with the boy and considered the issue of his freedom settled. Olympia was a mere "village," the editor wrote, as he pretended to be shivering with terror at the threat of "annihilation" by a U.S. Navy warship. The Victoria proceedings were perfectly legal, and attempts to undo them mocked the Declaration of Independence statement that "all men were created equal." Victoria would never be a "rendezvous for slave-catchers" because there was no slavery on the soil of the British Empire, anywhere in the world. The *Victoria Colonist* described Charles as "a bright, intelligent lad [who has] received some education" and concluded that Justice Cameron's judgment to free him was "a righteous decision."

Charles Mitchell had walked out of the courtroom and into the welcoming black community of the British Crown Colony of Victoria. That first giddy night, he certainly went to one of the local churches—or to the home of William Jerome or some other prominent black Victorian, perhaps Mifflin Gibbs or Wellington Moses—for an evening of celebration. Surely there was a feast and prayers and singing, with dozens of men and women, black and white, hugging the boy, shaking his hand, and wishing him well. Just three days before, on Sunday, he had been a lonely black child, a 13-year-old slave in a white household in Olympia. Monday morning, he had fled as a stowaway. Tuesday night, he had slept in a Victoria jail cell. And Wednesday night, he was a hero. Charles Mitchell was dizzy with freedom.

"You're free now, Charles Mitchell. Let me shake your hand!"

It seemed like a hundred people had gathered at the church hall in Victoria to celebrate Mitchell's freedom. It was noisy and hot. As he looked around, every face was smiling and kind, and nearly everyone was black. He had never seen so many black people at one time in his whole life.

"How do you feel?" everyone kept asking, grinning.

He felt great. Tired, sure, but great. For the last three days, he'd been so excited, so keyed up, that his very bones seemed to vibrate in his body. That had passed. When they had all walked out of the courtroom, cheering, Charles felt like he'd awakened from a long nightmare. He looked around clearheaded and curious—so this was Victoria. This was home.

Tonight, he felt joyful and solemn—and grateful. James Allen and William Davis had risked a lot to free him. James had lost his job—a good job, cooking on the steamer—and they probably couldn't ever go back to Olympia or Seattle. Tilton and his friends would be vengeful and on the lookout. In Washington Territory, James and William could be beat up or shot or lynched—they'd just disappear and their bodies would never be found. Charlie would never forget what he owed them.

Charles had a plate of fried chicken and biscuits in his hand, and he was suddenly very hungry. He smiled and then laughed out loud for sheer pleasure, and everyone nearby laughed with him. He was free. He could do anything. The big adventure was beginning.

8

TILTON'S CHOICE

It was midnight on a winter night in Olympia, 1861, and James Tilton was still awake, writing in his study. The oil lamp cast a circle of light on the desk and the rest of the room was in shadow, the mantel clock ticking, the household asleep. He glanced up as the wind lashed rain against the window. Tilton stared at his own reflection in the window pane, the gusting rain shivered his image, but then he saw his face clearly: thin, determined, worried. "I am not very well, nor have I had good health all the winter," he wrote to a friend. The injuries he had suffered in the Mexican War had stayed with him, chronic discomforts that sometimes grew worse. Of more concern, however, was the well-being of his country. "My family is as usual," he continued. "I will not talk to you about the deplorable state of our national affairs."

The "deplorable state" was the election of Abraham Lincoln to the presidency and the subsequent secession of southern states. Two months after Charles Mitchell fled Washington Territory, Americans voted in the crucial presidential election of 1860. As a resident of Washington Territory, Tilton had been unable to vote, and he watched anxiously from the sidelines as the Democratic Party split over slavery, nominating two presidential tickets. Tilton's friend Isaac Stevens had gone east to manage the campaign of John Breckenridge, presidential candidate on the pro-southern Democratic slate. Tilton doubted that Breckenridge could win, but he couldn't bring himself to support the northern Democratic candidate, Stephen Douglas.

This deep split in the Democratic Party opened the door for Abraham Lincoln, the Republican nominee, who was swept into office. Like many pro-southern Democrats, Tilton was convinced that Lincoln would not protect slavery in the South or permit its expansion to the territories. In response to Lincoln's election, South Carolina seceded in December, quickly followed by six other southern states. The Confederate States of America was formed in February 1861, and disunion became a reality.

In his March 4, 1861, inaugural address, President Lincoln tried to win back the seceded states and reassure the undecided ones, stating, "I have no purpose, directly or indirectly, to interfere with the institution of slavery in the States where it exists. I believe I have no lawful right to do so, and I have no inclination to do so." Many Democrats, including Stevens and Tilton, advocated a national convention to revise the Constitution to protect slavery and avert civil war. But hopes for reconciliation faded and opposing perspectives hardened, especially after Confederate forces fired on federal troops at Fort Sumter, on an island off Charleston, South Carolina. On April 15, 1861, President Lincoln took the U.S. forces into civil war against the Confederacy to put down rebellion and enforce the Union.

Picking up his pen, James Tilton continued his letter: "Of course we are all for the union here." Tilton was affirming that he and his friends in Washington Territory did not favor disunion but also did not support "coercion," as southern sympathizers described military measures to punish the seceded states and force their return. Tilton denied any federal power to limit slavery—he was convinced that the Constitution protected slavery as an individual property right and authorized the states to manage their own affairs. Above all, Tilton detested Lincoln and the Republican Party as fanatics willing to destroy the Union over the issue of slavery. The times demanded decision. As a man who had lived in the borderlands between slave and free—Maryland and Delaware, Indiana and Kentucky—Tilton faced a hard choice: to stay loyal or go south.

In Washington Territory, Tilton was often described as "a southern gentleman." Local Republican newspapers like the *Washington Standard* smeared all such Democrats who had migrated from southern or border states or spoke with a southern accent as rebels. The newspapers repeatedly urged "these traitors" to leave the territory and "seek their secession friends in the 'sunny south.'" In fact, some of Tilton's southern Democratic friends and fellow appointees had already chosen to leave Washington Territory for the Confederacy. Territorial governor Richard Gholson had resigned to work for Kentucky's secession, refusing "for even one day to serve under a so-called Republican president." Other friends had left the territory, but Tilton missed three in particular: George Pickett, Edmund Fitzhugh, and Isaac Stevens.

Capt. George Pickett had fought at Chapultepec alongside Tilton in the war with Mexico and then had commanded the U.S. troops on San Juan Island during the so-called Pig War. Pickett married a Haida woman who died not long after the birth of their son, James Tilton Pickett, named in honor of the men's close friendship. Pickett chose to resign his U.S. Army commission and head back to Virginia to fight for the Confederacy. He left his 3-year-old son in Washington Territory to be raised by a local family, and Tilton pledged to support the boy.

Edmund Fitzhugh had invested with Tilton in the development of Sehome and the Bellingham Bay Trail. Then Fitzhugh had helped Isaac Stevens run southern Democrat John Breckinridge's failed campaign for the presidency against Lincoln. Like Pickett, Fitzhugh was from Virginia and left behind his Native family in Washington Territory. Fitzhugh, too, decided to leave and join the Confederate Army. He served in Pickett's division.

Isaac Stevens and Tilton were both civil engineers, veterans of the Mexican War, stalwart Democrats, and friends. They had both fought and been wounded at Chapultepec. They had worked side-by-side throughout the Washington Territory's Treaty War and were advocates for the transcontinental railroad. Stevens was a firm proslavery, pro-southern Democrat, but after South Carolina troops fired on Fort Sumter, his choice was clear: to put down rebellion. Stevens requested and gained a colonel's commission in the Union Army. Tilton and Stevens had had their differences over the years, but it was widely rumored that Stevens's decision to fight for the North broke their friendship beyond healing.

Four friends, four choices. Tilton did not follow Stevens into the Union Army, nor did he follow Fitzhugh and Pickett into the Confederate Army. He chose to stay in Washington Territory. In public he claimed to be both an antiwar Democrat and a loyal American. But throughout the Civil War, Tilton was accused by his political enemies of holding more extreme private opinions—of being a rebel, a secessionist, a conspirator, a traitor, and a copperhead (a new word applied to sympathizers with the Confederacy). Defending himself, Tilton chose to fight his own war, a war of words. It was a bold choice and a stubborn one; James Tilton's war was one of deep conviction.

When Lincoln was elected, Tilton knew that he would lose his job as surveyor-general. Because he was a Democrat, Tilton would soon be replaced by a Republican, chosen by the president. When Anson Henry was appointed, the name-calling began. The *San Francisco Daily Evening Bulletin* published an anonymous letter that applauded the arrival of the new surveyor-general in September 1861, stating that Henry's appointment "will kick out of office a band of secessionists and traitors who have long been living on the Government. For some time it has been a thorn in the side of the Union men here, that the Government should retain its enemies in office, who openly and constantly . . . advocate their treasonable doctrine."

In Olympia, the *Washington Standard* complained about the

influence of "dissatisfied Southern office hunters and ambitious politicians . . . on the Pacific Coast"—ridiculing out-of-work Democrats like Tilton who remained in the territory. In fact, there were frequent sarcastic references to old Pierce and Buchanan appointees who hung around, drinking Tilton's "good whiskey" and hatching schemes for their political comeback.

Although land surveying was his profession, Tilton had become a political man. He was definitely interested in running for territorial delegate to the U.S. Congress in 1861. But the Democratic Party convention in Washington Territory instead chose Seleucius Garfielde, and Tilton "bolted" the party to protest the nomination. Speaking "as a patriot, a lover of the Union and a Democrat" in the *Puget Sound Herald*, Tilton attacked Garfielde as dishonest and untrustworthy and not a "real" Democrat. In turn, the Democratic *Union Flag* accused Tilton himself of not being a "real" Democrat but instead "as strong a secessionist as there is in the country . . . who sympathizes with the Southern Confederacy and is one of their principal apologists in this Territory." Some went so far as to accuse Tilton of being a Knight of the Golden Circle, the secret society that advocated establishing a slavery empire with Cuba at is center.

For years, some westerners had argued that the Far West—Washington, Oregon, and California—had little in common with the United States. The nation fell into two unequal pieces: a strip of territory along the West Coast and the states back east, separated by a vast and unforgiving geography. The West looked to Asia; the East to Europe. Above all, the West had gold and the East had none. Every two weeks, a steamship left San Francisco with nearly $1 million in gold mined in California but bound for eastern banks. Territorial newspapers frequently reported gold strikes in the Pacific Northwest. In fact, Hanson Tilton—James Tilton's younger brother—was reported in October 1861 to be panning $2,000 a week in the Cariboo country in British Columbia. Why not secede, asked advocates, and form a new Pacific Republic?

That dream matched the agenda of the shadowy Knights of the Golden Circle. The Knights had originally organized in the East, and there had been a chapter of the paramilitary group at the Latta Tavern, outside Dupont, Indiana. The Knights chapters, or "castles," that organized during the Civil War argued that the western states should not only secede but join the southern Confederacy. There may have been only two or three dozen members of the group in western Washington Territory, but the new Republican governor, William Pickering, was deeply concerned about the threat posed by the Knights, whom he called "these Barons, Lords, Earls, Dukes and Princes of Rank Treason."

John Murphy, editor of the *Washington Standard* and a supporter of the new Republican surveyor-general, frankly accused James Tilton of treason, one of those who "do not like to be called secessionists or traitors, [but] sail under the old banner of democracy." Murphy pointed out that Tilton had been a Breckenridge supporter during the 1860 election and claimed that "Breckenridge Democrats turn to secessionists as naturally as tadpoles to frogs." Then an anonymous Olympia correspondent sent a letter to the *San Francisco Bulletin*, bluntly calling Tilton a "traitor and secessionist." Tilton shot off a volley of letters to both newspapers, protesting hotly that while he was "no supporter of Mr. Lincoln's administration," he was not a traitor and would "gladly bestow [his] heart's blood" to reestablish the Union "in its original strength and unity." Unlike abolitionists, he wrote, he was unwilling to destroy the United States for a principle.

Murphy's insults escalated. The editor described Tilton's public letters as "disloyal effusions" and urged "Mr. T" not to sit out the war in Washington Territory but to join his Confederate friends in "the land of Dixie." The battle of words came to a head in October, 1861, when Tilton swore a loyalty oath to the United States before an Olympia notary public, a requirement of any man receiving a pension, as he did for his Mexican War wounds. Murphy published the oath word for word, scoffing at Tilton's hypocrisy in signing it.

"Sir, you make the mistake of a partisan in supposing that a citizen may not exercise his judgment, voice or vote upon questions of the administration of the Government, and yet be a true . . . citizen of the Republic," Tilton wrote back with heat, struggling to explain how a man could be loyal to the Union but disagree radically with the Lincoln administration. He claimed the right to be a "loyal citizen opposed to rebellion, abolitionism, military despotism and all violations of the constitution of the best government of the best republic yet made by man."

But how, countered Murphy scornfully, during a civil war, could a *loyal* American possibly oppose the president who was committed to ending the rebellion? No, Murphy concluded, Tilton was a greedy, cowardly, lying traitor. Goaded beyond endurance, Tilton retorted that Murphy was a sneak and a coward and should be horsewhipped for his slanders and for doubting the "honor of an old soldier." If Murphy was a man of courage, he would meet Tilton in a duel "to vindicate his personal honor." Having successfully baited Tilton into a fury, Murphy mocked his impassioned challenge to a duel and declined, joking that one or the other man might actually get hurt.

In February 1862, Tilton had a chance to prove his loyalty. He was offered the appointment of lieutenant-colonel in command of the regiment of the U.S. Volunteer Infantry in Washington Territory. Though Tilton continued to be publicly described as sympathetic to the Confederacy, his battle experience, personal courage, and commitment to the territory were beyond question. "An Old Comrade of Tilton's" wrote a letter to the editor of the *San Francisco Bulletin*, noting that "the commission could not have been bestowed on a worthier gentleman or a more gallant soldier." But Tilton, after working hard to gain the position, was too ill to accept it, "his health seriously impaired by injuries contracted during his military service in Mexico." For the rest of his life, Tilton was troubled by spells of sickness that confined him to bed.

Then, in September 1862, the news of Isaac Stevens's death in battle reached Washington Territory. On the battlefield at Chantilly, in Virginia, Stevens had lofted his regiment's fallen flag and charged toward the Confederate enemy. He was shot in the head and died on the battlefield. More than most, James Tilton knew what war was really like—the dust and noise, the fear and anger, the sweat and blood, the great wild chaos of battle brought into instant focus by one act of bravery or one mistake, one sword thrust or one bullet. Tilton was deeply grieved for the man who had been his comrade and friend, from whom he had parted on bad terms. Once, it was thought the Civil War would never begin; then, that it would be over in six months. But by Thanksgiving 1862, the war had "assumed a stern reality." It seemed as though it would never end. For reasons unknown but surely related to illness, grief, and torment, James Tilton disappeared from public life for more than a year.

In the summer of 1863, a wan James Tilton turned into Clancy's Saloon and headed for his customary table in the shadows. As he settled himself, Tilton groaned, stretching out his right leg, and shook his head wearily. Seated with his back to the wall, he gestured to the bartender, "The usual, if you please, Mr. Clancy."

An hour later, Ed Huggins, retired from the Hudson's Bay Company, came in from the bright sunlight, his eyes dazzled. "Over here, Mr. Huggins," called Tilton. "Come, sit down and have a brandy with me." He gestured once more for Clancy.

As Huggins settled in, Tilton lowered his voice, "You know it won't be long now, Mr. Huggins. This terrible ordeal has to end soon. Robert E. Lee is a military genius, and George Meade is timid and incompetent. If General Lee can keep the federal armies bottled up, spending their men, public opinion in the North will drive Lincoln to the bargaining table. You'll see—you can't believe everything you read in the papers—they're controlled by the Republicans. Gettysburg was a Confederate victory—I'm waiting to get a letter from George Pickett. Lee can take Washington, DC, if he has to, even Philadelphia. The Confederates are valiant men, and they're fighting for their homes, their families, and their way of life."

"Sounds like you wish them well, Mr. Tilton."

Tilton's voice hardened. "There are times, if it weren't for my bad health, I'd leave all this behind and join my friends in the South."

Huggins shifted in his chair and raised a shaggy eyebrow. "Why would you do that?"

"A society that permits black equality is doomed, Mr. Huggins. Blacks should know their place, and they shouldn't associate freely with whites. White gentlemen have the responsibility to protect their wives and the family. Free Negro labor will drive the white working-man into poverty. I want no part of this new nation Lincoln speaks of."

Huggins rose slowly from his chair and lifted his empty glass. "Thank you, Mr. Tilton, for the brandy."

9

JAMES TILTON'S WAR

Across the vast American continent from Washington Territory, in the year 1864, the Civil War was grinding on. General William Sherman had rested his troops in Atlanta and was continuing his punishing march through Georgia. Hundreds of thousands of blue-and-gray-clad soldiers had already been killed on the battlefields or died from their wounds or disease in crude military hospitals or miserable prison camps. In Victoria, southern sympathizers carried on a battle of symbols with abolitionists, raising more Confederate flags over the Crown Colony than patriots raised Union flags. Free blacks in the city cheered President Lincoln's Emancipation Proclamation from afar and thought of returning home, someday. The following spring, in 1865, Charles Mitchell turned 18, a free man in Victoria, and, after a year of silence, James Tilton returned to the political fight in Washington Territory.

One foggy morning, Tilton walked down the hill from his house and onto the wooden sidewalks of downtown Olympia. He opened the door to the new *Washington Democrat*, where editor Urban Hicks was busy setting type. Tilton had invested in the *Democrat*, helping the editor purchase the old press and type of the *Puget Sound Herald* and transport the equipment from Steilacoom to Olympia. There had been no Democratic newspaper west of the Cascades for more than three-years—it was time to start one again.

The office was a meeting place for Democrats, a place to catch the latest news from the East. The new telegraph brought bulletins almost instantaneously to Washington Territory. Lincoln had won a second term, and that was a disappointment to Tilton but no surprise. The bell jingled over the door and Tilton greeted a friend—in all, half a dozen local Democrats walked in during the next few minutes, gathering at the newspaper they had revived with their "generous liberality." Over a bottle of brandy, amid a cloud of cigar smoke, they planned their strategy to send a Democrat as territorial delegate to the U.S. Congress in 1865. The longer the war dragged on and the more men died, the more likely a Democratic victory would be.

A political man needed a newspaper as his voice, and James Tilton once again had a voice in the *Democrat*. The previous spring he had lost the race for Thurston County representative to the territorial legislature, but he soon gained the position of chief clerk of the Territorial Council and was elected treasurer by the legislature. Then the Democrat-controlled legislature appointed Tilton president of the University of Washington's Board of Regents. The territory's Republican press casually labeled all the regents "copperheads," referring to those Democrats who opposed the Lincoln administration and advocated a negotiated settlement of the Civil War. "Copperhead" was an insult, intended to slander any antiwar Democrat as a traitor.

If he was a copperhead, Tilton was not alone in the greater Pacific Northwest. Though Victoria sheltered a substantial black community—it was Charlie Mitchell's new home—it was also "a hotbed of secessionists, many of whom had been driven from the U.S. on account of their disunion sentiments," according to the *Victoria Colonist*. Throughout the war, Confederate agents in Victoria were reported to be outfitting warships to cruise in the Pacific and also encouraging Native attacks in Washington Territory. Territorial newspapers reported a steady stream of fist-fights and petty acts of vandalism by Confederate partisans—a U.S. flag set on fire in Vancouver, bullets fired through the window of an abolitionist's home near Chehalis, ugly words scrawled on a fence in Seattle. In Olympia, at a Fourth of July picnic, someone placed a cake on the dessert table, beautifully frosted and decorated with a perfect Confederate flag—the Dixie Stars and Bars at a Washington Territory picnic while the nation was at war. Not every pro-southern Democrat had "gone south."

In the second year of war, the issue of slave emancipation came to the fore, hardening the racial views of Democrats like Tilton. Shortly after his election, Abraham Lincoln had identified slavery as the fundamental issue that had driven the Confederacy to rebellion. He wrote to a southern correspondent, "You think slavery is right and ought to be extended, while we think it is wrong and ought to be restricted." Lincoln took the North to war to restore the Union, but as the dreadful years dragged on, abolishing slavery slowly became a central issue of the war. In an executive order issued January 1, 1863, President Lincoln ordered all slaves set free in the ten remaining states of the Confederacy—the Emancipation Proclamation.

Congress had already freed all slaves in the territories of the United States in June 1862. This resolution might have freed Charles Mitchell in Washington Territory, but it may not have applied to slaves who still belonged to owners in slaveholding states not in rebellion, such as Maryland. When Charles ran away, Tilton had claimed that the boy was only *employed* by the Tilton family but was actually the slave property of Maryland resident Rebecca Gibson. If Charles had remained in Washington Territory, his status would have been unclear.

Even though Charles might not have been affected by the resolution or by the Emancipation Proclamation, they marked a profound change in the reasons for the Civil War. Many territorial settlers thought the United States was now committed to eventually ending slavery everywhere. The Emancipation Proclamation was a strategic effort to weaken the Confederacy, but it also indicated that the war continued for different purposes than it had at its beginning. The shift was clear to newspapermen in Washington Territory. "The question now," editorialized the Democratic *Walla Walla Statesman* in 1863, "is whether this war is to be prosecuted for the sole purpose of putting down the rebellion . . . or for destroying slavery regardless of the consequences to the Union."

The Emancipation Proclamation confirmed James Tilton's conviction that the North had always intended to free the slaves and would go even further to institute black equality—actions he bitterly opposed. Sitting in a saloon in Olympia, Tilton had spoken quietly to Edward Huggins over a few glasses of brandy, but once the war was openly fought about slavery and race, he chose to speak more loudly.

Although Tilton didn't write every word in the *Washington Democrat*, the newspaper reflected his convictions, "a frank, manly, open avowal of principles" with "no beating about the bush." Basically, the *Democrat* editorialized, the framers of the Constitution intended *white* men to be equal citizens, not *all* men, and they had established a government of white men to represent their sovereign states. The *Democrat* appealed to the "sons and daughters of liberty-loving, patriotic white men" to remember that Abraham Lincoln—"in the fourth year of a bloody rebellion"—still refused to negotiate with southern peace commissioners unless they pledged to abolish slavery.

The *Democrat* published scurrilous, racially tinged gossip about Lincoln, for instance reporting that "Old Abe" was seeking a divorce from his wife to "take unto himself a sable wench" and begin the "great work of miscegenation," and much more. Tilton's newspaper railed against black equality, warning against social relationships between black and white, black wageworkers competing with whites, and the political dangers of black citizenship.

Tilton's immediate goal was to gain the Democratic Party's nomination as territorial delegate to the U.S. House of Representatives, the nomination he had lost in 1861. From the start, however, his candidacy was doomed. Gen. Robert E. Lee surrendered the Confederate Army at the Appomattox Court House in Virginia, on April 9, 1865, and the Civil War was finally over. Less than a week later, a band was playing a concert of "lively airs" to an Olympia crowd, celebrating the kick-off of Tilton's campaign, when a telegrapher rushed to the stage and handed a note to the conductor. The music changed to a dirge, and the announcement was made to the crowd: "President Lincoln has been assassinated."

Notice of Tilton's nomination by the territory's Democratic convention was published in the April 20, 1865, issue of the *Washington Democrat*, but it was completely overshadowed by news of Abraham Lincoln's assassination. The announcement of Tilton's candidacy, like everything in the newspaper on that day, was edged with the black of mourning.

In the wake of Confederate surrender and the shocking assassination, the nation and Washington Territory rallied behind the Union Party, composed of Republicans and Democrats who had supported Lincoln's war policy. Tilton's outspoken opposition to the Lincoln administration weakened his chances in the territorial election. His opponent was Arthur Denny, an abolitionist and son of John Denny, friend and colleague of President Lincoln. Lincoln's martyred death drew a cloak of dignity and righteousness around Denny. Every insult that the *Washington Democrat* had published about Lincoln—and there were many—came back to haunt Tilton's candidacy.

The newspaper campaign was furious. The two Democratic papers in Washington Territory—the *Washington Democrat* west of the Cascades and the *Walla Walla Statesman* in the east—loyally championed candidate Tilton, praising his political connections in Washington, DC, and his Mexican War service. Tilton's enemies countered that he was at best a shameless opportunist, calculating and ambitious, and at worst a traitor. One San Francisco reporter joked that "for four years [Tilton] has been waiting for 'something to turn up,' and he has finally 'turned up' this nomination for delegate to Congress."

Tilton's spokesmen defended him, admitting that he had originally been an office-seeking presidential appointee but that he had remained in the territory, built a home, and raised a family. "He intends to live and die a citizen of Washington Territory," said his supporters. Tilton was no opportunist who might do or say "anything, everything, to suit the occasion," but a principled man—an "unflinching Democrat" who had consistently "opposed both secession and negro equality."

Tilton's Republican and Unionist opponents labeled him old-fashioned, behind the times, a "fossil politician" who should have remained a "staid, unobtrusive and harmless old fogy," whose "private opinions, however antiquated or odious" could then easily have been ignored. Democratic newspapers protested that Tilton was loyal and that Isaac Stevens, a Union hero who had died at Chantilly, was Tilton's "old friend and comrade." The Republican *Seattle Gazette* retorted that Tilton and Stevens's friendship had fractured over the men's wartime allegiances. Further, claimed the *Gazette*, Tilton remained friendly with Confederate officers George Pickett and Edmund Fitzhugh, using the outlawed mail service between the Pacific Northwest and the seceded states to keep in touch. The wartime choices that Tilton made crippled his political chances in 1865.

In May 1865, the Democrats of Washington Territory waited for Tilton to take to the campaign trail, to confront his accusers and challengers. But Tilton was sick in Olympia, confined to bed with pneumonia. The Democratic newspapers and Tilton's spokesmen carried on, warning that Arthur Denny and the Unionists would "sustain Negro equality . . . to create what they term a 'New Nation.'" In fact, Tilton's antiblack rhetoric was probably his strongest asset in Washington Territory, where slavery was almost universally condemned but there was little sentiment in favor of black equality.

At the very end, James Tilton's former slave, Charles Mitchell, became part of the campaign. The candidate's spokesmen argued that Tilton demonstrated his "abstract" position on slavery by bringing "a negro boy" to Washington Territory to train him as a "steamboat steward" and then to free him. Tilton's supporters claimed that he had brought the boy west as an act of compassion, intending from the start to emancipate him. But Tilton never said that he opposed slavery on principle. On the contrary, he had long insisted that only states had the power to emancipate slaves. He was strongly opposed to federal actions that emancipated slaves and elevated freed blacks to social, economic, and political parity with whites. He believed in a hierarchy of race in which whites were superior and blacks, Mexicans, and Indians were inferior.

Tilton's complicated relationship with Charlie Mitchell was a web of inequality, of power and obligation, where the black boy was expected to defer to the white man's authoritarian, fatherly plan for his life. In fact, many territorial Democrats believed that Tilton's racial views were enlightened—certainly George Pickett named his mixed-race son James Tilton Pickett to honor Tilton and place the boy securely in his care. Charlie's refusal to submit to Tilton's plan confirmed the older man's fears for the future. Charlie's flight was Tilton's personal experience of the future that the Civil War was fought to build.

In a letter published in the *Washington Democrat* a week before the election, Tilton lamented "the New Nation" that would arise out of the war. "I was satisfied with the old union," he wrote, "and would have sacrificed anything and will still do so to preserve and perpetuate our old form of Government." But Tilton lost the election to Arthur Denny by a landslide, and the *Democrat* ceased publication six weeks later.

The ambitious young man who had stepped off the steamer at the Olympia dock in 1855 had become an "old Southerner" by 1865, a political failure loyal to a lost cause. A war and the loss of 600,000 lives liberated 4 million slaves. The Thirteenth, Fourteenth, and Fifteenth Amendments to the Constitution decisively ended slavery, identified black men as citizens, and give all male citizens the right to vote. During Tilton's campaign for territorial delegate, his supporters claimed he would live and die in Washington Territory. But Tilton and his family left Olympia behind on October 16, 1865, and headed back east, leaving his mixed-race namesake James Tilton Pickett behind. James Tilton picked up the pieces of family life and his surveying profession but never again participated in politics. As the steamer chugged away from the dock in Olympia, Tilton did not look back.

Two men sat idly on a drift log on the beach, tossing pebbles toward the water.

"Well, there goes James Tilton and the wife and kids. The cook, the dog, and the cat—but not the slave or the shirttail relatives . . . How the mighty have fallen!"

"He got a pretty rough handling in the election, poor old guy."

"And now he's heading back east with his tail between his legs. No, he don't get much sympathy from me. I remember when he brought his whole damn family out here, and you couldn't turn around without tripping over one of them. Gave 'em all the good jobs too. Surveyors, my foot."

"You weren't here during the Indian war. Tilton really knew what to do, compared with most of these desk soldiers. He got us guns and he got us paid—though that took a while. He was a hero in the Mexican War, you know."

"Who cares? You're always looking back, you and all them Democrats. That was twenty years ago. I'm more interested in what happens next, here in the territory. Telegraph's already here, and railroad's sure to come soon. Republicans did that for us."

"And who do you think did the surveys for the railroad in the first place?"

"Well, I don't know and I don't care. Good riddance, I say! Probably be more political hacks just like him next time there's a Democrat in the White House."

10

CHARLES MITCHELL'S PEACE

In the years that followed his escape, Charles came to know his new home. When he arrived in 1860, Victoria was an exciting international boomtown, three times the size of Olympia. "Shrewd, thrifty, intelligent" men were aggressively trying to get rich by mining the miners who were all headed up to the goldfields. Less than a week before his arrival, nearly $35,000 in gold dust had arrived from the Fraser and Thompson River goldfields on a single steamer, bound for the Victoria assay office. Even though gold fever was slowly winding down, hundreds of hopeful miners still pulsed through town, pacing along Victoria's muddy streets, waiting for steamers bound for the north.

Charles was surprised by the number of people of color in Victoria. Of three thousand residents, about a quarter were black, born in Britain, Jamaica, Barbados, and the United States. The port thronged with Hawaiians, Chinese, East Indians, Chileans, Mexicans, Americans, and Europeans of every nation who spoke a dozen different languages. Compared with Olympia, Victoria was an international city, and it was truly exciting to live there.

Victoria's streets, boulevards, and public squares were oriented to the bustling harbor, pulsing with commerce. Ships of every description crowded the port, bringing cargo from all over the world. The town boasted churches, schools, government halls, a number of brick buildings, and some fine homes. There was a scatter of elegant hotels, fine restaurants, and ornate theaters and a rowdy red light district.

Charles was a teenaged schoolboy. He moved into a warm and loving home in Victoria's black community and began to attend the Collegiate School for Boys on Church Way. His tuition—$6 per month—was paid by his new friends. The school promised a solid English education "designed to qualify [students] for the learned professions, commercial and mercantile pursuits, and for the universities." The teachers taught the boys science, or "natural philosophy," mathematics, penmanship, and modern languages like French, German, and Spanish and the ancient languages, Hebrew, Greek, and Latin.

Unlike the schools he attended in Steilacoom and Olympia, Collegiate educated the sons of the city's elite. In March 1861— when Charles had been a student for six months—two English-women toured the school and met the boys. One penned a brief glimpse of Charles Mitchell among his classmates: "a very nice looking set of boys—in rank, from the Governor's son, downward. There are not more than 2 or 3 coloured boys & even those are not very dark. One however is a fugitive slave, a boy whose history excited a good deal of attention in these parts. He was most kindly treated by his master and mistress, of whom, stories of their cruelty to him, were circulated to their great pain. He is not particularly intelligent."

After their visit, the ladies donated a portrait of the Prince of Wales and some books to the school and continued on their journey. Their note is the last certain bit of evidence of Charles Mitchell's life, and it is intriguing and frustrating. The ladies' white hosts in Victoria had gossiped with their English visitors about the black boy and his story. They would have told their guests that James and Belle Tilton felt "great pain" at hearing stories of their cruelty to the boy and that the couple maintained he had been "most kindly treated" in Olympia. One of his teachers would likely have remarked to the ladies that Charles was "not particularly intelligent." The ladies themselves observed that he was "not very dark," which made him "nice looking," by their standards. But above all, he was a "fugitive slave . . . whose history excited a good deal of attention." That was how Charles Mitchell was best known, for his past and for the decision he had made. He had made his choice; he was no longer a slave, and so his story changed.

On clear days, from a spot on Victoria's Beacon Hill, Charles could have seen the far Olympics and the Cascade Mountains, all the way south to Mount Rainier. Among scudding clouds and passing rain squalls, ships entered Victoria harbor from Olympia and Honolulu, from San Francisco and London. Groups of Native canoes threaded their way through the harbor. For months after his escape, the *Eliza Anderson* arrived weekly. Captain John Fleming and first mate Woodbury Doane could be seen walking around on board or striding up and down the dock. At first, Charles probably hid from them, staying away from the harbor when the mail steamer was in port. But he would have eventually stopped worrying about them. Charles knew they had no power over him; he was free. The world spread out before him.

Growing up in Victoria, he likely discovered the city was not without challenges for a young man of color. He became just another young black man in a city on the downward slide from the gold rush boom. By the mid-1860s, antiblack discrimination became widespread as secessionists from the United States flooded the city. During the war, Confederate flags had flown from hotels and taverns in Victoria, and afterward many "rebels" did not wish to return to the "New Nation."

Although churches and schools were open to them, Victoria's blacks were never called for jury duty and were denied service in some shops run by American immigrants. At the Civil War's end, Victoria's black population fell dramatically. Many, like the successful black merchant Mifflin Gibbs, returned home to the United States, eager to claim places in a more egalitarian postwar society. Undoubtedly, some of the men who had helped Charles to flee the Tilton home in Olympia returned to the United States, eager to see old friends in the New Nation.

After 1861, Charles Mitchell almost vanishes from the historical record. At the end of the Civil War, he might have remained in Canada. Better educated than most young men of color, he could have become a clerk or even a surveyor or the steward James Tilton had envisioned, baking bread and basting chickens on a Puget Sound steamer. Perhaps he joined the British Royal Navy and sailed the world's oceans as Tilton had done or prospected for gold, up in the mountain streams of British Columbia. Or, as Washington Territory grew steadily in population and trade, Charles might have returned to work in Olympia or its rival port, Seattle.

"Charles Mitchell" is a common name, and in censuses of the 1870s there are two dozen young black men of that name scattered throughout the United States and Canada. After the Civil War, Charles was free to return to the United States without fear, and it makes sense that he would try to find his family. He may have tried to locate his father. A white man named Charles A. Mitchell, age 22 and described as a "mariner," was listed in the 1850 U.S. census in Dorchester County, which neighbored Talbot County where the Marengo Plantation was located. Thirty years later a Charles Mitchell, white, age 52 and described in the census as a "seaman," was living in California. It is possible that if Charles could have traced his father, he would have visited him, and that meeting may not have been a happy one. However, the odds are great against the young man ever finding his footloose father, if he had even wanted to meet him.

There is, however, an intriguing piece of data in the 1870 census. A black Charles Mitchell, birthplace Maryland, age 23, was listed as living in the same Baltimore household as a black woman, Rebecca Mitchell, age 46. These ages closely match the ages of the small black boy and young black woman who were part of the Marengo household in 1850. After the Civil War, the former slave woman might have stayed on as a hired servant to the Gibsons until they could no longer afford her. Then, like many freed men and women, she would have left to seek work in the nearest city, Baltimore. Perhaps she took the last name of Mitchell rather than Gibson to help Charles find her. After sixteen years of separation from his family, Charles was free to head home to Maryland to search for his "Aunt Becky."

The tall, light-skinned young man kneaded his felt hat between his hands as he stood on the front steps, waiting for Mistress Gibson to come to the door. At least, that's what he used to call her long ago at Marengo. She had been forced to leave the plantation, and so had he. She was living where he left her—in the town of St. Michaels, in a house much like the one Charles Mitchell and his family lived in back in Victoria. It was a simple townhouse on a quiet side street that ran down to the bay and the oyster packing plant there. The smell of shucked oysters lay heavy on the hot August air. He had traveled a long road from Victoria, on Vancouver Island, to this town on the Chesapeake Bay in Maryland, and he was weary.

Rebecca Gibson opened the door and paused, looking warily at the stranger who had knocked so insistently in the midday heat. Something in the turn of his head, the look in his eyes, awakened the memory of a sad young boy who had listened so quietly when she told him he must go west.

"Charlie?" she said with a question in her voice, taking one step toward him.

Charles Mitchell made no move forward. "Yes. I've come to find my aunt," he said, with a faint hint of British precision in his voice. "Is she here?"

"Becky came to town with me, but she didn't stay," she replied, struggling to find the words to answer this serious young man, so grown up now, so abrupt in his manner. "She was always loyal. She didn't leave until the very end, but there was no work here. I couldn't pay her. You remember—we had to sell it, sell Marengo. And it's all gone." She looked off across the Miles River to the neck of land on the distant shore.

"What happened to everybody? All the people—where'd they go?"
Rebecca Gibson drew herself up. "Them? They've gone away." She
sighed.

Charlie shifted from one foot to the other. "And my father? Where
is he?"

"I don't know nothing about that man," she replied, her voice ris-
ing. "No-account waterman. You just leave that be." She didn't ask
Charlie to sit down or if he wanted some water. Just stared hard at
him, studying him, looking for the child he'd been, trying to figure him
out. "Where've you been, Charlie? We heard you run off . . ."

"Yes'm. Left Mr. Tilton and set out for Victoria. Got a wife now,
got a house. Working in the woods. Times are tough but I wanted to
see Aunty Becky again, so I came all this way . . ."

"You might try Baltimore," she said. "They most all went to the
city." A seagull screamed overhead, then another and another, and
she glanced up. "He came back, you know—Jim Tilton. Back from the
west. He and Belle did, and the whole family—I guess they're up in
Delaware, at Tilton Hill. But everything is all so different now."

"Yes, it is. It is different." Charlie looked at the gulls, too, and then
at Mistress Gibson. She was thinner, older, wearing a dress that he
almost remembered, now threadbare and faded. She didn't meet his
gaze, just kept staring away, away from his face.

"Well, I guess I'll try Baltimore then." He nodded and turned to go,
lifting his bag.

"Charlie!"

"Yes'm?"

"She calls herself Becky Mitchell—don't know why she didn't use
my name, like the rest of them. Ask around in Seton Hill. Heard that's
where she's gone."

"Thank you, Miz Gibson."

She smiled vaguely and closed the door.

EPILOGUE

Free Men

What really happened to Charles Mitchell? The historical evidence is slim. He does not appear again in a census in Baltimore or Victoria after 1870. If he reunited with his aunt, Mitchell may have spent a year or two with her in Baltimore but returned to Victoria to stay. He probably felt more at home in Victoria than anywhere else. Black men named Charles Mitchell appear in the historical record around Victoria a couple of times after the Civil War. In one newspaper report, a "colored man named Charles Mitchell" left the logging community of Sooke with a white man and a canoe laden with cedar shingles on Sunday, February 13, 1876. Five days later, the canoe and some of the shingles washed up twenty-five miles southeast on shore at Beachy Bay at the foot of Church Hill, but there was no sign of either man. A second canoe sent out to search for them found nothing. This Charles Mitchell left a wife and three children and a fourth born after his death. This is most likely the Charles Mitchell who fled James Tilton in September 1860—and who died at 29 years of age, in 1876.

Whatever his life and however it ended, Charles Mitchell made a bold choice for freedom in September 1860, risking everything to gain the right to choose and work for his own future. His brief moment in history was his assertion of independence, the first, last, and only known fugitive slave to travel the tiny Puget Sound Underground Railroad.

At the end of 1865, James Tilton returned briefly to Indiana to visit his home and family—a pilgrimage of sorts. He had been soundly defeated at the polls in Washington Territory, his patriotism had been repeatedly called into question, and the society in which he lived and in which he believed had been destroyed by the Civil War. At 46 years of age, he was a man adrift, his place insecure in the nation under a Reconstruction that Abraham Lincoln had envisioned and died for.

Tilton's brother Mark had married and prospered as a banker and pension agent in Madison, Indiana. His sister Rebecca was raising a family there. But whatever Tilton was looking for, Indiana proved a disappointment. Tilton was no farmer and not much of a businessman, and the state no longer held opportunities for a surveyor. As an outspoken Democrat, he had no reason to expect government appointments from the Republican administration. So, instead of settling down on the family land in Dupont, Tilton moved his family back to Tilton Hill, in Wilmington, Delaware—the original Tilton home.

James Tilton didn't linger in Wilmington either, for he had a large family to support and was a man of restless ambition. The West drew him back when the Northern Pacific Railroad offered him a job in Washington Territory using his skills and extensive knowledge of the mountain passes he had mapped. Tilton was hired in 1867 to survey the route for the Northern Pacific and determine a suitable pass through the Cascades for the great transcontinental railroad, the settlers' dream finally a reality. He stayed for six years, surveying the Walla Walla & Columbia River Railroad, laying out the new railroad town of Newaukum, and developing a preliminary town plan for New Tacoma, which became the Puget Sound terminus of the Northern Pacific.

Ever in search of construction projects in the postwar nation, Tilton returned east in the mid-1870s to work as a civil engineer on the public works of Georgia and improvements to the upper Coosa River. Then he contributed to the daring canal effort to connect the Mississippi River from Cairo, Illinois, through to

Darien, Georgia, and on to the Atlantic Ocean. Finally, Tilton took a position as inspector of the Washington, DC, waterworks, and the family moved to that city with him. James Tilton died there at 60, in 1878.

After his death, Isabella Tilton tried to pull his legacy together. As the widow of a wounded Mexican War veteran, she filed affidavits to maintain her husband's pension and drafted letters to establish his importance in building the Pacific Northwest. Her sons were dispersed throughout the continent. The oldest, Edward, surveyed a railroad in Peru. The youngest, James, worked as a revenue agent in New Jersey. A third son, Howard, settled in Seattle. Isabella herself returned to Washington to settle disputes over property the Tiltons owned there. This time she stayed in the far Northwest, living the rest of her life in a rooming house in Victoria. By the time she died in 1896, the Northern Pacific Railroad had been completed to Puget Sound, and Washington had become a state.

James Tilton had assumed responsibility for supporting an extended household, a role that made sense to him in the prewar social hierarchy. He took care of his widowed sister and her family; found jobs for his brother, sons, and nephews; assisted his mother's family in Maryland; and extended his sense of obligation and ownership to a half-breed Haida boy and a young black slave. He knew, Tilton did, what should become of Charles Mitchell—he should learn to cook and when he was of age, he should go to work as a steward on a Puget Sound steamer. Tilton never got over the ingratitude of the black boy who rejected this paternalistic vision.

So ends the story of two free men: one whose freedom and place in society had been secured by tradition and one whose freedom and place in society had been denied by tradition. James Tilton and Charles Mitchell had been as white to black, man to boy, owner to slave, guardian to ward, employer to employee, benefactor to dependent, and even, some said, as father to son. Whatever their precise relationship, whatever bonds of obligation joined them, they lay somewhere along the spectrum of slavery and were only severed by Mitchell's insistence on making his own future against Tilton's will.

These two men—slave and master—demonstrate the mutually degrading effects of slavery. Mitchell's identity was determined by his birth to an enslaved black woman, and the boy's decision to run away forced Tilton to explicitly state that he regarded Mitchell as property. Charles Mitchell had to abandon his life and gamble his future to gain his freedom, and James Tilton's sense of worth depended, at least in part, on his power over Charles Mitchell.

Their individual stories also reflect the bitter inequalities of race, the injustices that plunged the country into the horrors of the Civil War and the uncertainties of Reconstruction. For Tilton, Charles Mitchell's flight and the war's outcome marked the end of a way of life in which James Tilton was acknowledged as a gentleman, powerful and paternal, at the top of a hierarchy of color. For Mitchell, his escape and the war marked the beginning of a new order in which James Tilton was humbled, in which Charles Mitchell was his own master and took his own risks.

ACKNOWLEDGMENTS

First we'd like to acknowledge this collaboration: two seasoned, strong-willed historians and authors researching and writing together on this book. Lorraine brought the idea, the skills of a research historian, and years of teaching and interpreting history to the public. Judy brought a diligence for tracking down genealogy, experience as a writer for young adults, and years of teaching both writing and history.

To interpret this story in its historical context, we were inspired by the work of many others in both fiction and nonfiction, in particular: Virginia Hamilton, James McBride, James McGowan, Esther Mumford, and Quintard Taylor.

We had the assistance of many librarians, historians, archivists, genealogists, and bibliophiles: Redmond Barnett, Jonathan Blitstein, Sharon Boswell, Pat Brady (and our other friends at the Puget Sound Civil War Roundtable), Rick Breithaupt, Jae Breitweiser, Theodore Brooke, Meagan S. Brown, Tamara Bunnell, Peggy A. Burge, Doug Denne, Ed Diaz, Ted Dusablon, Roger Easton, Jodee Fenton, Susan Goff, Meredith Gregg, David Hastings, Elbert Hinds, Susan Karren, Kyra Kester, Candace Lein-Hayes, Stephanie Lile, Karen Maeda-Allman, Lou Malcomb, Tracy McKenzie, Ed Nolan, Julie Petit, Carla Rickerson, Orlando Rideout V, Jean Russo, Shanna Stevenson, Sarah Stolte, Carl James Tilton Jr., Frederike Verspoor, Cynthia Wilson, and Candace Wellman.

Thanks to the Seattle Public Library for providing the writers' room; to Allen Bentley for his conference room with a view; and to Rob McConaghy, Jeff McConaghy, and Peter Bentley for wise counsel on many aspects of the book. Thanks to writers Kate Willette, Stephanie Guerra, Janine Brodine, Susan Starbuck and Christine Castigliano for very helpful feedback. Most of all, we thank editor Marianne Keddington-Lang for her early and persistent enthusiasm and support, Julie Van Pelt for attentive but gentle copyediting, Ashley Saleeba and Tom Eykemans for design guidance, and Gregory Christie for adding an artistic interpretation to the history.

METHODS AND SOURCES

Free Boy attempts to present a balanced biography of two men, a master and a slave whose lives were intertwined but for whom the existing evidence of lives led is very unequal. It is fairly easy to research James Tilton; it is very difficult to research Charles Mitchell. This little-known story of a boy who escaped from slavery in Washington Territory challenges complacency about the state's racial history, and so we have tried to write a narrative that will appeal to a wide range of readers. We have combined traditional historical biography with historical reconstruction, dispensing with endnotes but including a full bibliography.

This biography roots Charles Mitchell and James Tilton in the context of their times, among real people, real places, and real events. Mitchell and Tilton lived and made choices in Delaware, Maryland, Indiana, Mexico, Washington Territory, and Victoria, British Columbia, during a sweep of time from the Mexican War (1846–48) through Reconstruction (1865–77). General histories of those places and times have given us an understanding of the shared experience of these two men, the master and the slave.

Because the historical record for Charles Mitchell is thin, we crafted dramatized scenes—printed in italics—to convey his inner life through dialogue, action, and reflection. The italicized encounters are entirely invented, but the people are real and their interactions are based on our research and understanding. For instance, Lewis Nesqually Bush, who we imagine talking with Mitchell in chapter 3, is a real boy of a similar age and race as

Mitchell, but whether they were friends is unknown. In contrast, the conversations of Edward Huggins and James Tilton during wartime are documented in correspondence, but the exact words of the two men are unknown and thus in italics.

Where there is a written record, the subjects—primarily James Tilton—speak in their own quoted words. That is, when Tilton's words are not italicized and are between quotation marks, those remarks are from correspondence or from published interviews or speeches. However, when such words are unavailable, we have appropriated attitudes typical of other American Democrats who served as military officers in the Mexican War, attitudes confirmed by Tilton's own words during his run for Washington's territorial delegate in 1865.

Charles Mitchell's escape is well documented, though the three chapters that deal with his flight also use creative license. For instance, we have imagined the food James Allen was cooking for breakfast and lunch on the *Eliza Anderson* and the serenade of Mitchell by Victoria's black community on September 25, 1860. After years of research, Mitchell is still more unknown to us than James Tilton. Mitchell lived a full life but left scant evidence, in part because he was born into slavery.

Even in the slave census of 1850, the first such count of enslaved people in the United States, the names of slaves are not listed, just their age, gender, and color (*B* for black; *M* for mulatto). The slave census for Marengo, the plantation where Mitchell was born, does include a mulatto boy who would have been the same age as Mitchell. In later accounts of Tilton's relationship to Mitchell, statements are made that the boy was 3 years old in 1850 when his mother died in the cholera epidemic and that her mistress promised to take care of the orphaned boy. Charlie is definitely listed by name in the federal census of 1860, living in Olympia with the Tilton family.

What is also known with certainty about Mitchell comes from the 1860 court hearing in Victoria and from affidavits, correspondence, and newspaper articles that concern his escape from

Washington Territory—the center of the story told here. Aside from one glimpse of Mitchell at school in Victoria in 1861, nothing more is known for certain about the rest of his life. There is no obituary in the Maryland, Washington, or British Columbia newspapers for a Charles Mitchell who is without doubt the escaped slave, nor did he leave a will.

For his life after 1860, we considered four pieces of potential evidence. One is the newspaper report of the lost canoe off Sooke in 1876 described in the epilogue. A second comes from the *Victoria Colonist* of August 29, 1861, which reported that "Charles Mitchell, a colored man" was arrested for "beating a squaw" on Kanaka Road. We don't think this is the same Charles Mitchell. Charles would have been only 14 years old at the time, very young to be considered a "man." It is also significant that—less than a year after the escape of Charles Mitchell from the Tilton home—he was not identified in this news article as the former fugitive slave. It makes sense that his backstory would still have been interesting news to the *Colonist's* readers and would have been included.

In the third instance, a man named Charles Mitchell was accused in 1883 of bludgeoning John Harris to death at Point Roberts, Washington Territory, a point of land that extends south from Canada into U.S. water. Witnesses described a squalid settlement of drunken, violent men and their Native women. In more than one hundred pages of affidavits and testimony, this Charles Mitchell was repeatedly called "the Greek" and never once referred to as "the Negro" or "the mulatto." At a time when local newspapers usually mentioned the race of those accused of a crime, the *Puget Sound Mail* reported the case and did not characterize Mitchell as black. Instead, in 1889, the *Blaine Journal* described Mitchell as "a Greek brigand." This Charles Mitchell was clearly swarthy, but he seemed more Greek than black to his contemporaries. Additionally, "Charley the Greek" was illiterate—unable to sign his name to his testimony, he made an *X* as his mark on court documents. Charles Mitchell the free boy was highly literate, educated in Olympia, Steilacoom, and at the elite Collegiate School in Victoria. We do not believe that the Charles Mitchell accused of murder is the Charles Mitchell whose life is the subject of this book.

The fourth piece of evidence is the 1870 U.S. census entry that places Charles Mitchell and Rebecca Mitchell together in a Baltimore house. We have depended on the census taker's accuracy in providing gender, race, and age—so much so that we argue that Charles Mitchell returned to Maryland after the Civil War to find his Aunt Becky and spent time with her in Baltimore. However, the enumerator also recorded that the young man was unable to read or write. There are many possible explanations for this: the census taker may have assumed that the young black man was illiterate, he may have been in a hurry and checkmarked the wrong line, he may have asked Rebecca Mitchell whether Charles Mitchell was literate and she may have answered that he wasn't. We don't know for sure, but we are convinced that despite the claim of illiteracy, the 1870 census documents Charles Mitchell's stay with his aunt Rebecca Mitchell.

Thus, the documentation for Charles Mitchell's biography is thin and unsatisfying; each primary source presents a set of problems. Future research may resolve these uncertainties, but this is the way we believe Charles Mitchell lived and died.

James Tilton is much easier to research because he was born to parents descended from prominent families and lived a public life. Both his mother's family (the Gibsons) and his father's family (the Tiltons) had property records and wills, and the family trees have been traced by genealogists. Newspaper coverage followed the Tiltons and Gibsons wherever they lived, and some family members had short biographies written about them. During his sixty years, James Tilton wrote correspondence, published letters to the editor in various newspapers, ran for public office, served in the military and received a military pension, and filed government reports on his work. This written record fully accounts for the various stages of his life, from family origins in

Wilmington, Delaware, to his father's founding of Dupont, Indiana; from service in the Mexican War to his wide-ranging career as a surveyor, naval officer, and a political man; and finally to his death. James Tilton the man emerges from a variety of sources.

The privilege that James Tilton enjoyed in life followed him after death; his paper trail is rich and full while Charles Mitchell's is thin and uncertain. This biography attempts to balance the story.

SELECTED BIBLIOGRAPHY

PRIMARY SOURCES

Newspapers

Daily National Intelligencer (Washington, DC)
Madison Courier (Indiana)
Northwest (Port Townsend)
Oregonian (Portland, OR)
Pioneer and Democrat (Olympia)
Puget Sound Herald (Steilacoom)
San Francisco Daily Evening Bulletin
Seattle Gazette
Union Flag (Vancouver)
Vancouver Register
Victoria Colonist
Walla Walla Statesman
Washington Democrat (Vancouver)
Washington Standard (Olympia)

Public Documents

Canadian Census, 1891. www.ancestry.com.
Jefferson County Apprenticeship Records, Smith, John, (R-285)
    March 1840 (colored). www.myindianahome.net/gen/jeff/
    records/apprent.html.

U.S. Census, 1800–1810, 1820, 1840, 1850, 1860, 1870, 1880. AncestryLibrary edition. www.ancestry.com.

U.S. Military Service Records, Pension Files. National Archives and Records Administration, Washington, DC.

U.S. Slave Census, 1850. National Archives and Records Administration, Seattle, WA.

Washington Territorial Legislature, Resolutions. Washington State Archives, Olympia, WA.

Maps and Surveys

Map of Lancaster Township. Jefferson County Indiana Plat Maps. S. W. Briggs & Co., 1876. Compiled by Jefferson County Historical Society.

"Report of Edwin F. Johnson, engineer-in-chief to the Board of Directors, Northern Pacific Railroad Company. Including Reports of surveys, executed in 1867 by Gen. Ira Spaulding, chief engineer of the Minnesota Division, and Gen. James Tilton, chief engineer of the Washington Division, Northern Pacific Railroad Company." Hartford, CT: Case, Lockwood and Brainard, 1869.

Tilton, James. "Map of a Part of the Territory of Washington: To Accompany the Report of Surveyor General." [Washington, DC: General Land Office], 1855.

———. "Map of a Part of the Territory of Washington: To Accompany the Report of the Surveyor General." U.S. Surveyor General, 1861.

———. "The Survey of the Walla Walla and Columbia River Railroad." Walla Walla, Washington Territory: Statesman Printing Office, 1871.

Archival Collections

British Columbia Archives, Victoria, BC
  Judicial Files

Digital Library on American Slavery
  Document number PAR 20483615,
  http://library.uncg.edu/slavery
Indiana Historical Society, Indianapolis, IN
  John Lyle King Diaries, 1842–79
Jefferson County Historical Society, Madison, IN
  "African Americans in and around Jefferson County." Type-
  script. N.d.
  Tilton Family History
Madison–Jefferson County Public Library, Madison, IN
  Tilton Family History
Oregon Historical Society, Portland, OR
  Knights of the Golden Circle
University of Washington, Special Collections, Seattle
  Eliza Anderson Collection
  Clarence Bagley Collection
  Richard Dickerson Gholson Papers
  McMicken Family Papers
  William Frasier Tolmie Papers
Washington State Archives, Olympia
  Isaac Ingalls Stevens Papers
Washington State Archives, Northwest Regional Archives, Bell-
  ingham
  Territorial Criminal Case Files, Records of the Whatcom
  County Clerk
Yale University Libraries, Beinecke Library of Western Ameri-
  cana, New Haven, CT
  James Tilton Papers
  William Winlock Miller Papers

OTHER PRIMARY SOURCES

"Emancipation Hymn of the West Indian Negroes, for the First
  of August Celebration." In *The Anti-Slavery Harp: A Collec-*

tion of Songs for Anti Slavery Meetings, by William W. Brown. Boston: Marsh, 1848.

Hoggatt, Brad, and Ruth Hoggatt. MyIndianaHome.net, 1996.

SECONDARY SOURCES

Asher, Brad. *Beyond the Reservation: Indians, Settlers, and the Law in Washington Territory, 1853–1889*. Norman: University of Oklahoma Press, 1999.

Bagley, Clarence. *History of King County, Washington*. Vol. 1. Chicago: Clarke, 1929.

Bancroft, Hubert Howe. *History of Washington, Idaho and Montana, 1845–1889*. San Francisco History Company, 1890.

Bauer, K. Jack. *The Mexican War, 1846–1848*. New York: Macmillan, 1974.

Blankenship, George E. *Lights and Shades of Pioneer Life on Puget Sound*. Olympia, 1923. Facsimile reprint, Shorey Bookstore, 1972.

Blankenship, Georgiana, ed. *Early History of Thurston County, Wa*. Olympia, 1914. Facsimile reprint, Shorey Bookstore,1972.

Breithaupt, Richard, H. *Aztec Club of 1847 Military Society of the Mexican War*. Van Nuys, CA: Walika Publishing Company, 1998.

Carey, Roland. "Trips of the *Eliza Anderson*." *The Sea Chest* 9, no. 1 (September 1975): 1–5.

Coon, Diane Perrine. *Southeastern Indiana's Underground Railroad Routes and Operations*. Indianapolis: Indiana Department of Natural Resources, Division of Historic Preservation and Archaeology, 2001.

Crenshaw, Gwendolyn J. "Bury Me in a Free land: The Abolitionist Movement in Indiana, 1816–1865." Indiana Historical Bureau, 1986. www.in.gov/history/2934.htm.

Davis, William. *John C. Breckinridge: Statesman, Soldier, Symbol*. Baton Rouge: Louisiana State University Press, 1974.

DeMeyer, Denny. "The Late Great Puget Sound Meridian." Land Surveyors' Association of Washington Historical Society, n.d. www.lsawhistorical.org/documents/articles_Puget-SoundMeridian.pdf.

Dustin, Charles Miar. *The Knights of the Golden Circle: The Story of the Pacific Coast Secessionists.* Chicago: Self-published, 1903.

Eckrom, J. A. *Remembered Drums: A History of the Puget Sound Indian War.* Walla Walla, WA: Pioneer Press, 1989.

Edson, Lelah Jackson. *The Fourth Corner: Highlights from the Early Northwest.* Bellingham, WA: Cox Brothers, 1951.

"Eleutherian College." National Historic Landmark Nomination, 1996. http://pdfhost.focus.nps.gov/docs/NHLS/Text/93001410.pdf.

Ellison, Joseph. "Designs for a Pacific Republic, 1843–1862." *Oregon Historical Quarterly* 31 (December 1930): 319–42.

Esarey, Logan. *History of Indiana.* Vols. 1 and 2. Dayton, OH: Dayton Publishing, 1934.

Etulain, Richard W. *Lincoln Looks West: From the Mississippi to the Pacific.* Carbondale: Southern Illinois University Press, 2010.

———. "Washington and Idaho Territories, 1861–1865." *Journal of the West* 16 (1977): 26–35.

Ficken, Robert E. *Washington Territory.* Pullman: Washington State University Press, 2002.

Foster, Charles J. "The Pacific Coast in the Civil War." Master's thesis, University of Washington, 1924.

France, Erik D. "The Regiment of Voltigeurs, U.S.A.: A Case Study of the Mexican-American War." Paper presented at the Palo Alto International Conference on the Mexican-American War, Brownsville, TX, February1994. http://sites.google.com/site/efrance23/theregimentofvoltigeurs,usa.

Gibbs, Mifflin Wistar. *Shadow and Light: An Autobiography.* 1902. Reprint, Lincoln: University of Nebraska Press,1994.

Grigson, Harry. *A History of Victoria, 1842–1970.* Victoria: Victoria Observer, 1970.

Hansen, David Kimball. "Public Response to the Civil War in Washington Territory and Oregon, 1861–1865." Thesis, University of Washington, 1971.

"James Tilton, WA Terr. Univ., 1864." *Washington Historical Quarterly* 13, no. 4 (October 1922).

Jeffcott, Percival. "Romance and Intrigue on Bellingham Bay; or, The Story of Old Sehome and the Origin of Its Name." N.d., typescript. Whatcom County Historical Society, Bellingham.

Johannsen, Robert W. *Frontier Politics and Sectional Conflict: The Pacific Northwest on the Eve of the Civil War.* Seattle: University of Washington Press, 1955.

———. *The Frontier, the Union and Stephen A. Douglas.* Urbana: University of Illinois Press, 1989.

———. "The Sectional Controversy and the Frontier: Pacific Northwest Politics on the Eve of the Civil War." PhD diss., University of Washington, 1953.

———. "Washington Territory and the Major Political Parties." Thesis, University of Washington, 1949.

Johansen, Dorothy, and Charles M. Gates. *Empire of the Columbia: A History of the Pacific Northwest.* New York: Harper and Row, 1967.

Josephy, Alvin M. *The Civil War in the American West.* New York: Knopf, 1991.

Kilian, Crawford. *Go Do Some Great Thing: The Black Pioneers of British Columbia.* Vancouver, BC: Douglas and McIntyre, 1978.

Kluger, Richard. *The Bitter Waters of Medicine Creek: A Tragic Clash between White and Native America.* New York: Knopf, 2011.

Knights of the Golden Circle. *An Authentic Exposition of the Origins, Objects and Secret Work of the Organization Known as the Knights of the Golden Circle.* U.S. National U.C., 1862.

Lang, William L. *Confederacy of Ambition: William Winlock Miller and the Making of Washington Territory.* Seattle: University of Washington Press, 1996.

Lapp, Rudolph M. *Archy Lee: A California Fugitive Slave Case*. San Francisco: Book Club of California, 1969.

Lewis, Oscar. *The War in the Far West: 1861–1865*. Garden City, NY: Doubleday, 1961.

Mahoney, Barbara. "Oregon Democracy, Asahel Bush, Slavery and the Statehood Debate." *Oregon Historical Quarterly* 110 (2009): 202–27.

McDonald, Lucile. "James Tilton, Territorial Surveyor." *Seattle Times*, May 25, 1958.

Meany, Edmond S. *Governors of Washington State*. Seattle: University of Washington Press, 1915.

Meeker, Ezra. *The Tragedy of Leschi*. Seattle: Lowman and Hanford, 1905.

Morgan, Murray. "Charles Was Young, Black, and Running." *Seattle Post-Intelligencer*, April 9, 1972, 4–5.

Mumford, Esther. "Slaves and Free Men: Blacks in the Oregon Country 1840–1860." *Oregon Historical Quarterly* (Summer 1982).

Muncie, Emery O. "A History of Jefferson County, IN." Master's thesis, Indiana University, 1932.

Newell, Gordon R. *Rogues, Buffoons and Statesmen*. Seattle: Hangman Press, 1975.

———. *So Fair a Dwelling Place: A History of Olympia and Thurston County, Washington*. Olympia: Warren's Printing and Graphics Arts, 1950.

Pilton, James. "Negro Settlement in British Columbia, 1858–1871." Master's thesis, University of British Columbia, 1951.

Preston, J. Dickson. *Talbot County: A History*. Centreville, MD: Tidewater Publishers, 1983.

Rathbun, John C. *History of Thurston County*. Olympia, 1895.

Reid, Robie L. "How One Slave Became Free: An Episode of the Old Days in Victoria." *British Columbia Historical Quarterly* 6, no. 4 (October 1942): 251–56.

Rosenberg, Charles E. *The Cholera Years, the United States in 1832, 1849, and 1866*. Chicago: University of Chicago Press, 1987.

Richards, Kent D. *Young Man in a Hurry: Washington's First Territorial Governor, 1853–1857*. Pullman: Washington State University Press, 1993.

Smith, Dorothy Blakey, ed. *Lady Franklin Visits the Pacific Northwest: Being Extracts from the Letters of Miss Sophia Cracroft*. Victoria, BC: Provincial Archives of British Columbia, 1974.

Smith, Justin H. *War with Mexico*. Vol. 2. Gloucester, MA: Peter Smith, 1963.

South Bay: Its History and Its People, 1840–1940. Olympia, WA: South Bay Historical Association, 1986.

Stevens, Hazard. *The Life of Isaac Ingalls Stevens*. Boston: Houghton, Mifflin, 1900.

Taylor, Quintard. "A History of Blacks in the Pacific Northwest 1788–1970." Thesis, University of Minnesota, 1976.

———. *In Search of the Racial Frontier: African Americans in the West*. New York: Norton, 1998.

———. "Slaves and Free Men: Blacks in the Oregon Country 1840–1860." *Oregon Historical Quarterly* 83, no. 2 (Summer 1982): 153–70.

Thrush, Coll. "'I See What I Have Done': The Life and Murder Trial of Xwelas, a S'Klallam Woman." *Western Historical Quarterly* 26 (1995): 168–83.

———. *Native Seattle: Histories from the Crossing-Over Place*. Seattle: University of Washington Press, 2007.

Tilghman, Oswald, and Samuel Alexander Harrison. *History of Talbot County, Maryland, 1661–1861*. Vol. 1. Baltimore: Williams and Wilkins, 1915.

"Underground Railroad Network to Freedom, the Story of Georgetown District in Madison, Indiana." Indiana Department of Natural Resources, Division of Historic Preservation and Archaeology, n.d. www.in.gov/dnr/historic/files/georgetown.pdf.

Vouri, Michael. *The Pig War: Standoff at Griffin Bay*. Friday Harbor, WA: Griffin Bay Bookstore, 1999.

Waddington, Alfred. *The Fraser Mines Vindicated*. 1858. Vancouver, BC: Robert R. Reid, 1949.

Wright, E. W., ed. *Lewis and Dryden's Marine History of the Northwest*. Portland, OR: Lewis and Dryden, 1895

Writers' Program of the Works Progress Administration. *Maryland: A Guide to the Old Line State*. New York: Oxford University Press, 1940.

Yonce, Fred. "Public Land Surveys in Washington." *Pacific Northwest Quarterly* 63 (October 1972): 129–41.